NO LONGER A BRIDESMAID!

I0157165

TERRY CATO

MAHOGANY INSPIRATION

Laveen, AZ 85339

ISBN: 978-0-9894644-0-6

Text copyright 2013 by Terry Cato. All rights reserved.

Published by Mahogany Inspiration

5045 W. Baseline Rd., Ste. 105-112, Laveen, AZ 85339

Library of Congress Control Number: 2013910434

Printed in the United States of America

Mahogany Inspiration, June 2013

Cover Design, Najwa Jai

Cover Design Edits, Diana Blackwell

This book is dedicated to the loving memories of my mom Barbara Ann Smith-Hunter and mother-in-law Dale E. Sullivan. May they both rest in heavenly peace.

CONTENTS

ACKNOWLEDGMENTS

A special shout-out and thank you to my loving husband Lloyd G. Cato, for supporting and believing in me from the very beginning – I love you more than I can verbalize; and my children for their understanding and patience as Mommy spent countless hours on the sofa with the laptop.

My content editor and soror, Dr. Sharese T. Willis, thank you for your initial feedback and assessment; I hope you are pleased with the final product.

My content and copy editor, Soror Monica Carter Tagore, thank you! Thank you! And thank you! I so appreciate your wisdom and direction from the very beginning.

To my dear friend, Alice, thank you for your prayers! I never asked, but I know you were praying for me – I felt it.

To my sister-in-law, Twila, thank you for planting the book seed in my mind years ago. I still remember you telling me, "Terry, you should put this stuff in a book!" ... Well, I finally did; praise be to God!

Bishop Rick and Deborah Garrett, senior pastors at Azusa South Mountain, thank you for your anointed marriage enrichment classes. This is where I received divine inspiration to outline the idea for this and future books.

And finally, last but definitely not least, a special thank you to my dear cousin, Paula. You gave me the book to read and the encouragement that started me on my path to preparing for my husband. I will forever be grateful to you for that. Thank you, may God repay you for how you have blessed my life, because I never could – love you to pieces!

FOREWORD

The best advice that I have for single women is to wait on God's timing; to not settle for anything less than God's best and to enjoy your single days.

Waiting is one of the most difficult things to do, whether we're waiting for a phone call, for a relationship to change, or for an answered prayer. But we have to remember that God's timing is different than our own and that His timing is *perfect*. Habakkuk 2:3 says, *"For the vision is yet for an appointed time; But at the end it will speak, and it will not lie. Though it tarries, wait for it; because it will surely come, it will not tarry."*

God sees things from a different perspective and sees the whole picture, not just what we want, but what is best for us in the grand plan for our lives. All is part of a divine order and will be done in its own right and proper time. God uses the waiting period to prepare us and our mates. Trust that He will bring the perfect person at the perfect time – when both are ready.

God also promises to do *"exceedingly and abundantly above all that you can ask for or think."* He knows the desires of our hearts, yet He promises to do above and beyond what we've asked for or can even imagine. Don't settle for anything less than God's best. So often in desperation, we settle for what appears to be the real thing. Always pray and ask for guidance and discernment from the Holy Spirit on whether the relationship you've entered into is the one that God has ordained for you. God will make it plain.

Your single years should be some of the best days of your life. You have the freedom to discover yourself and the world. Live those days to the absolute fullest and in the words of Bishop T.D. Jakes, "get ready, get ready, get ready" for what God has for you.

Minister Paula T. Wright

INTRODUCTION

Most girls at some point fantasize about their wedding day. For me, I always dreamed of having an intimate, exotic wedding with a beautiful beach as the backdrop. My fantasy started out as a simple ceremony with a few close friends and relatives. Over the years, the fantasy of my dream wedding became bigger and more elaborate. One thing, however, always remained the same – the beautiful body of water as the backdrop. The wedding I fantasized about was very different from my actual wedding day.

My wedding day is one I will never forget. I was surrounded by close family and friends. It was a small, intimate ceremony at a local wedding chapel – the day was absolutely beautiful and was filled with many emotions, ranging from overwhelming excitement to great sadness. I was overjoyed that I was finally about to marry the man of my dreams yet sad because my mother was not there to share in the merriment of my wedding day. My mother went home to be with the Lord on June 28, 2000—nearly five years before I said, "I do." Although she was not there physically, I somehow knew she was there in spirit.

My personal journey of becoming a bride didn't start December 25, 2004, the day I became engaged. My journey to become a bride had begun several years earlier when I made a commitment to myself and God that I would begin preparing myself for my husband. In this commitment, I made a vow that included abstaining from casual dating and premarital sex, taking some time to work on becoming the best me, and beginning to get to know and love me so that I would enter marriage a whole individual for the person I would marry.

Approximately 7 years after I made this vow, on April 2, 2005, I took my walk down the coveted bridal aisle—starting the day as a single woman and ending it as a married one.

My reason for writing this memoir, *No Longer a Bridesmaid!* was to memorialize and share what God has done for me. I want my testimony of preparing to be a bride, wife, and mother for seven years to be an encouragement to the many others who are waiting and preparing for their Boaz. There is no need to get weary in waiting. As you wait keep your eyes focused on the prize, and completely lose yourself in Christ. Become the best you that you can be – become someone who is lovable, more importantly become someone who can love unconditionally.

My journey is a display of faith and a walk of patience. If God did it for me, He can and will do it for you.

"He who finds a wife finds a good thing,
and obtains favor from the Lord."
Proverbs 18:22(NKJV)

PART I: MEET THE SINGLE LADIES

CHAPTER 1

YOU'RE CALLING ME A WHAT?!

I've had the blessed opportunity to share my testimony of preparation with many single women. As a result of my sharing with these women, the door to relationship dialogue usually opens and over the years, I've heard relationship horror stories, success stories, and everything you could imagine in between. I began to notice similar characteristics in these women and soon found myself starting to categorize the single women that I come into contact with.

The women came from varying backgrounds, but they shared many similarities. The most common characteristic was that the vast majority were Christian, and most had formal/post secondary education. All appeared to be hardworking, success-driven women. And without a doubt, most everyone had the "infamous list!"

In categorizing these single women, I came up

with seven primary categories to describe the relationship personalities of single ladies that I've come across. There is a chapter dedicated to each personality, describing the characteristics of that group and the potential dilemma or pitfall that could keep these single women in a state of singleness; exception being, the Lady-in-Waiting chapter. The pitfalls of the Lady-in-Waiting are there as a precaution since the Lady-in-Waiting is a single lady who is actually engaged to be married.

Some single ladies may fit the characteristics of more than one category. And others may find themselves in one category and over time fit the characteristics of another. The latter best describes me. I started out as the Professional Student with a bit of the Church Sister stirred in; over time, I became a hard core Church Sister before becoming a Lady-in-Waiting.

The purpose of this book is to bring to light the various personalities, not that any particular personality is good or bad, but to see the personality for what it is and move forward to a place of being a Lady-in-Waiting, if that is what the single lady desires!

CHAPTER 2

THE PROFESSIONAL STUDENT

Professional Student– 1) Person who receives multiple degrees and keeps taking courses instead of holding a profession related to the degrees earned. 2) Someone who goes to school with no specific reason in mind or goal; someone who likes going to school; someone who never wants to graduate.[1]

The Professional Student is always either in school working on a degree or taking classes toward some sort of certification. It is highly probable that the Professional Student does not work in the field that she has spent time and money getting educated in. Nonetheless, she has made a commitment to educate herself to the point where she has no time to date, be in a serious relationship, or much less, get married. She

---

[1] *UrbanDictionary.com*

feels very few men are on her level intellectually and prides herself in her education and superior IQ.

This single lady knows all the ins and outs of college life and is a wonderful resource for students who are a little green when it comes to college life. Her motto is, "You can never have too much education."

Her ideal mate has at least two degrees and is well certified with various professional designations. He has attended an Ivy League or top tier institution—anything else simply will not do. If he graduated magna or summa cum laude, that is a definite plus. He must make more money than she and his credit must be A++. He is well-cultured, well-travelled, and well-spoken. His family consists of a long line of educators and education administrators. So ideally, her mate is NOT a first-generation college graduate.

Pitfall: The pitfall of the professional student is that she has created this "dream man" who potentially does not exist for her to justify the fact that "there simply are no good men out there." When I was single, I would always find myself in the company of other single women who would throw these pity parties and talk about how there were no good men available and that all the good men were already married. At that time a lot of these women, like myself, were in graduate school. Based on my observation of these women, I truly believe that for many of them graduate school was a distraction – a way for them to not focus on their state of singleness. Their conversation always revealed that deep down inside they desired to be married. This theory was confirmed for me when I analyzed the results of a single ladies survey that I conducted and one of the respondents stated that she categorized herself as the Professional Student, "because right now I do not want to think about a husband or marriage; career bound." Her comment summarizes what several single women who categorized themselves as a Professional Student shared.

I also observed the Professional Student justifying her fleshly desires for a mate by stating, "God knows the desires of my heart." The Professional Student has to realize that God wants to bless her spirit, not her flesh. The Professional Student must also realize that there may be a man she is totally compatible with, who may not necessarily fit some of the fleshly desires of her heart; but may be someone who she is totally compatible with and someone who can grow with her. She must dig deep and prioritize her "list" and determine which qualities are truly important and the qualities that may be desirables, but are not must-haves. She needs to look for the items on her list that are not deal breakers.

Another young lady responded to the following survey question: "If you had to put yourself into a category, which would it be and why?" She said, "Professional Student because I went to school to become a licensed nurse, real estate no license obtained, insurance no license obtained, Bachelor's degree in Business Administration, and currently working on a Master's degree in Elementary Education."

Another respondent stated, "Professional Student because staying fruitful and keeping a fruitful mind will keep me focused and my mind off of the lonely dream of what most women look forward to, marriage, kids, and vacations."

There is nothing wrong with a woman getting a good, solid education; however, for the Professional Student personality, education can be an excuse for some to not move on in life and pursue other goals. For others, it is a security blanket to avoid delving into a career for fear of failure. The Professional Student must deal with any issues that may be causing her to delay moving on in life.

Finally, the Professional Student must realize that school and the pursuit of an education is not a substitute for companionship. Nothing can take the place of having a companion in our lives; God knew this. In the Bible in Genesis 2:18-22 (NKJV), God saw that it was not good for man to be alone. Every animal and every beast of the field had a companion, but there was no suitable companion for man. God created woman for man.

CHAPTER 3

THE CAREER WOMAN

"I think my generation of professional women are sort of waking up and realizing that we potentially may not be able to have it all, not at the same time."

~ First Lady Michelle Obama

The Career Woman has devoted herself to her career. She is literally married to her job. She will often be the first to arrive at the office and one of the last to leave. She has invested much time, money, and resources into her education so that she can advance on the fast track in her career. The career woman typically does not want to sacrifice her career for marriage or a family since she has so much invested in her vocation. She sometimes carries the dirty little secret that she is up to her ears in debt from trying to live a lifestyle that she cannot afford but feels she deserves. The Career Woman and Professional Student share many of the same personality traits, but their escape outlet sets them apart—a career for one and school for the other.

Regarding a relationship, the Career Woman will usually date, but will not remain in a relationship for long periods of time. There are many reasons for this. In fact, there is one that I have heard many times over, "This relationship requires [required] too much of my time. My schedule is just too busy right now to be bothered with a relationship."

I have come across more Career Women than I can count. And it never fails, her ideal mate is well-educated, has a six-figure income, is tall, handsome, and athletic; he has no kids and has never been married. These women have consistently shared an almost identical list of the characteristics that their ideal mate should possess — I am no longer surprised at this phenomenon. Additionally, her ideal mate has already attained what she is aspiring for—money and power, which means that he will obviously make more money than she.

Additionally, I've met many single career women who always want to know, "Can I have it all?" Meaning, can they have a successful career, marriage, and family at the same time. I personally believe that this lingering question in the mind of many career women, has made them hesitant to commit to even wanting to be married, for fear that they will somehow not be able to successfully manage having a career and family. I further believe that some of these women have even set the bar so high for their ideal mate that they have made it almost impossible to find this perfect man, this man we all know does not exist. When asked, "Why are you single?" A single lady who responded to a survey that I conducted stated, "Because I have standards and when a man approaches me he has to meet or exceed those standards; they seldom do."

A lot of Career Women I have met, share that in their twenties they were optimistic about marriage and having a family; then for those who are in their thirties and have never been married or have children find themselves progressing in their career and over the years their priority shifted to a place where their job became more important than their desire for a husband or family. This was even more evident in the Career Women who were in their late thirties and early forties.

One particular Career Woman who comes to mind shared with me that for her, she had been waiting too long for a husband to compromise on her list. Despite her age and the fact that she wanted children, she would always tell me that God promised to give her the desires of her heart. I was sometimes baffled by this particular woman because many of the characteristics of a mate that she desired, she did not possess. For example, she was adamant that her potential mate should be athletic and in good shape, she however, was a little overweight and hated the gym. Additionally, she had a significant amount of debt and frequently paid her bills late; her desire was that her mate would have good credit.

Another Career Woman shared with me that she had a major wake-up call at a friend's wedding. As she participated in and witnessed her friend get married she realized that she was not getting younger and she really did want a husband and children. She also thought long and hard about what this would mean for her career, being that she was a mid-level director in her company and had witnessed how working mothers were treated. This particular Career Woman is not alone. I have met many mid-level managers and directors like her. She is now happily married with children; and is a working mother. She did make adjustments to her career for the sake of her family by accepting a position with a different company that allowed a flexible schedule to accommodate her family life.

Pitfall: It's obvious that the Career Woman has married her career. The major pitfall of this personality is that at the end of the day her career cannot greet, hug, kiss, or make love to her. A career can never take the place of meaningful companionship in your life. Humans were born social beings; meaningful interaction with a significant other is not only needed, but is required for total fulfillment. When God made Adam, He saw that Adam—although a complete being—NEEDED companionship. So, He took a rib from Adam, wrapped flesh around it, gave this new being the feminine characteristics of the man, and Adam called her woman, translated "male" with a "womb" (Genesis 2: 18, 20, 23 NKJV). The Career Woman, like the Professional Student, must realize that nothing can take the place of companionship.

Switching companies or changing careers may

not work for everyone, but something that a Career Woman might want to consider, if her career path and/or company are not family friendly. Sacrificing her career is probably the one thing most Career Women have vowed they will not do, and I am not suggesting that she do this, however, I do suggest that the Career Women earnestly seek God for direction and decide that she will wholeheartedly follow where God leads.

The Career Woman must realize that her ideal mate just may not be as tall, athletic, and handsome as she prefers; however, if he meets her core criteria and not all of her fleshly desires will she not consider this person? The Career Woman must dig deep and prioritize what is truly important to her concerning traits her mate must possess.

And lastly, I suggest that the Career Woman who is holding out for her perfect mate, use her season of singleness to prepare herself to be the perfect woman that her perfect man will desire.

CHAPTER 4

DADDY'S LITTLE GIRL

Writing this chapter posed a unique challenge for me. I do not have a close relationship with my biological father. Actually, I have no relationship with him. For reasons unknown to me, other than my mother and father decided they would go their separate ways when I was about four and my twin brothers were babies, I have no idea why my father chose from that point on to not have any contact with his wife and small children. I therefore, personally have no first-hand knowledge of what it is like to be a daddy's girl. I have only observed other ladies either describe themselves or other people describe them as being a Daddy's Little Girl.

My observation of the Daddy's Little Girl personality was that this lady was oftentimes the spoiled brat of the family and there was nothing that her father would not do for her. And this was well known by the daddy's girl and all who knew her, since a typical statement by the daddy's girl would be, "my daddy is going to … or my daddy will do … for me." I sometimes cringed at those statements, either because I cannot relate to this at all or because these statements always came across as somewhat needy to me.

I have relied on the testimony of other ladies to illustrate the dynamics of a father-daughter relationship. My research revealed that most of these ladies grew up in a two-parent household and they generally had a good relationship with both parents, but were simply closer to their daddy. As one lady stated, she can go to her dad and talk about anything without him being judgmental. In comparison to her mom, whom she could talk to, but felt that her dad tended to be more understanding, and less likely to judge her; more than one lady stated this dynamic of their relationship with their father. Another quality that the daddy's girls mentioned was that their fathers were their protectors, the disciplinarian, or the enforcer; a couple of the ladies shared a similar scenario of when they were children and were with both parents, if they were shy and wanted to hide, they would hide behind their father. Another mentioned that anytime she was hurt, she always ran to her father.

The relationship that these ladies have with their fathers has impacted how they view men overall. One lady stated that her father and grandfather had such an impression on her growing up that she thought that all men were like them: honest, God-fearing, kind, and hardworking – now that she is older and has dated, she realized not every man possesses those qualities that she admires in her father and grandfather. Another lady stated that because of her father she feels that every man should be the primary provider for his wife and family.

These ladies all stated that their close relationship with their father affected how and whom they chose to date. Several ladies shared that they will not even consider some guys because they have a standard in place. One lady shared that she chose to not date one guy because he smoked and another because he drank – her father did not smoke or drink; and this was a total turnoff for her. Something I found interesting was that all of these ladies shared that their fathers had given them advice concerning what type of guys they should date and most heeded this advice. There was the occasional rebellion, where a couple of ladies admitted to dating guys who were nothing like what their father advised them to look for in a mate. For both of these ladies, they admitted that as they've matured, they realized that their father's advice on men and dating was the right advice.

Another perception that I have of the Daddy's Little Girl is that she is simply on a mission—that is, she wants to marry her father. This perception is not erroneous at all. Every one of the ladies that I spoke with thought very highly of their father and they desired many of same qualities in their mate that their fathers possessed. There is nothing wrong with a daddy's girl desiring the same characteristics in her mate that her father possesses if she is looking for those positive attributes that she admires in her father. However, sometimes the daddy's girl seeks out the negative attributes of her father, even though she often does not realize this. For example, I know of a young lady who has a close relationship with her father and was constantly in abusive relationships and didn't know why she continued to attract the same kind of violent men. After counseling, she came to the realization that her father had been physically and verbally abusive to her mother and she subconsciously was attracting the same kind of men for herself. Through Christian counseling, this young lady realized the dysfunction she witnessed as a child and is now married to a wonderful, loving man who adores and respects her.

Pitfalls: The primary pitfall that the Daddy's Little Girl should be aware of is to not eliminate a good man as a possible mate because he may not possess certain qualities of her father. This will take maturity and holy discernment for the Daddy's Little Girl to pick and choose what qualities are important to her and not compromise on attributes that are must-haves. Additionally, the Daddy's Little Girl must be careful to not compare her husband to her father. She must realize that although her husband and father may possess many of the same characteristics, they are two different people. The Daddy's Little Girl should never tell her husband what her daddy would do in a particular situation as if to rebuke or scold her husband. This could be detrimental to not only her husband's self confidence but to the marriage as well.

Equally as important, the Daddy's Little Girl will have to be careful that she does not subconsciously attract men who possess the not-so-stellar characteristics of her father. For example, another young lady was consistently dating men who were unfaithful to her. She began to question her mother about the reason for her parents' divorce. She learned that her father was indeed a "ladies' man," and the marriage had ended due to infidelity. And she was subconsciously attracting the same kind of men. This was an aha moment for her, and she now knew the innate source of her attraction to the type of men she was dating. Over time, this lady was able to heal from past hurts caused by infidelity and move forward in her process of preparing for a husband.

In closing, my research on the Daddy's Little Girl has revealed that most, if not all, little girls want to be adored and cherished by their father; and further these girls are watching their fathers and are looking for the qualities in their men that their father possesses. And for those girls who are lacking this sort of attention, some become grown women who crave attention — any attention — from a man, even if it means being abused.

For those ladies, who like me did not have their father in their life and cannot relate to being a Daddy's Little Girl, I share what I did to form a healthy view of a man. Being that my father was absent during my childhood, I only knew things about his personality that my family told me. I, therefore, looked for positive male role models in my church and community. I observed positive characteristics in my childhood pastor as well as other men in my church and school that I observed over the years. For most of the men I observed, I not only observed the man, but his wife and children. In my adulthood, I observed qualities in men who were a part of a longtime, stable marriage.

My observing men who carried themselves in a manner that I respected greatly impacted my list of characteristics that I desired in my husband. Characteristics that were at the top of my list included: God-fearing Christian, honest, and hard working. Those characteristics were some of my must-haves, qualities that I would not compromise on.

CHAPTER 5

THE SINGLE PARENT

"Single parent" is a term that is mostly used to suggest that one parent, who is not married, has most of the day-to-day responsibility in the raising of the child or children. And in most situations, the one parent is usually the mother.

God's original design for the family was that there be two parents in the household. Unfortunately, for many families, various circumstances such as divorce, death, and out-of-wedlock births prevent God's perfect desire for the family, and the sad truth is that many households are being headed by a single woman.

In 2006, 12.9 million families in the U.S. were headed by a single parent; 10.4 million single-parent mothers and 2.5 million single-parent fathers. Since 1994, the percentage of U.S. households headed by a single parent has remained steady at around nine percent, and is up five percent since 1970. Statistics show that there is an overwhelming number of single-parent mothers.[2]

Many Single Parents have been married and are divorced. God never intended for the family to be this way. God created man to not only have dominion over the earth, but to be the head of the household (Genesis 1:26, 28 & Genesis 2:24). As Christians, we live in a fallen world and have succumbed to the ills of a society that operates contrary to what God has ordained for His people. And sadly, it appears that Christian marriages are no more secure than those who are not of the faith. Marriage polls have shown time and time again, that Christians have a higher rate of divorce than non-Christians.

For divorced Single Parents, they must contend with a unique set of circumstances that could potentially complicate their decision to move forward and marry again. A primary issue being custody of their children and a close second is the financial responsibility of each parent as it relates to the child. I personally have witnessed situations where the mother is the primary custodian of the child(ren) and is about to remarry, and the ex-husband has an issue with the new man. And another situation where there were unresolved issues with the ex-husband that were

---

[2] U.S. Census Bureau, Families & Living Arrangement: 2006.

exacerbated by the fact that the ex-wife was about to remarry. In both of these situations, whether or not the issue was warranted is not the point. The point is that this ill behavior created problems in what were already stressful situations that involved young children; then the added stress from the ex-husbands. Not knowing all of the intimate details of these situations from all parties involved, I cannot argue for or against the ex-wives or ex-husbands. My advice, however, is to be mature about the matter and obviously always act in the best interest of the children involved.

I further suggest to the single woman who is a divorcee and is ready to re-enter the dating and marriage arena to work through any and all issues that she may have with her ex-husband. You never want underlying issues with a previous spouse to hinder your moving forward. And additionally, you never want to be the problem. The same maturity that you expect from your ex-husband concerning your decision to move forward and remarry, should be reciprocated if your ex decides – and I'm sure at some point he may – that he wants to remarry.

The Single Parent who is a widow obviously does not have an ex-spouse to factor into the equation when they are ready to re-marry. The widow's primary focus must be to completely heal from the loss of her spouse and in her own time decide when and if she will re-enter the dating scene. One such widow that I know, was married for 20+ years, has adult children, and has stated that she has no interest in remarrying again – she is only interested in a friend with shared interests that she can attend social events with. She shared that she is of the age where she is content being single and has no need for a husband. This Single Parent is in a good place that some may envy. She has experienced a longtime marriage, has adult kids, is financially secure, and is content in her state of singleness.

A widow who responded to my survey shared that she was interested in remarrying, but if she didn't remarry that was fine as well. She is a single parent of teenage children and actively dates. She too is content in her state of singleness. And what I have observed of her situation is that she is still grieving the loss of her husband. Although she dates, she does not expose her children to every man she goes out with. Since her husband's death, she has introduced her children to one man whom she has been dating steadily.

And then there is the Single Parent who has had a child or children out of wedlock. This Single Parent sometimes has issues that are parallel to those of the divorced single parent – custody and financial issues. The single parents who responded to my survey had the common thread of the divorced single parents, that their children were their number one priority and were the motivating factor in their decision to date or not to date. These mothers tended to be a bit more optimistic in their outlook of marriage when compared to the mothers who had been divorced.

The Single Parent faces many issues – not just the decision to marry or remarry. In many cases, the one parent is the sole provider responsible for the social, emotional, and financial stability of her child(ren). And most have no help in terms of babysitting responsibilities, household chores, and other tasks that need to be done to keep a household together.

Other research suggests that the children of single parents may be at a higher risk of poverty than children of two-parent homes. This particular study also contends that single mothers have poorer health than mothers who are married.[3]

Another study suggests that many factors influence how children develop in single-parent families – these factors include: the parent's age, education level, occupation, the family's income, the family's support network of friends and extended family members including the non-resident parent, if available. The study asserts that disadvantages in these factors that often accompany single parenting appear to cause most of this association rather than single parenting itself.[4]

As a Single Parent, whatever the circumstance, choosing to marry or remarry is never an easy decision, as there are children to consider. My advice for the single mother is to earnestly seek God in prayer as it relates to your decision to marry, especially considering

---

[3] Millar, Jane and Ridge, Tess (November 2001) 153 "'Families, Poverty, Work and Care: A review of literature on lone parents and low income couple families'" (DWP Research Report No.153) Leeds, CDS.

[4] Mackay, Ross (2005) "The impact of family structure and family change on child outcomes: a personal reading of the research literature" Social Policy Journal of New Zealand (accessed February 18, 2008).

the additional factors that must be considered, including ex-husband, children, stepchildren, and financial responsibility of the children.

In summary, my research of Single Parents revealed that many are hesitant to move forward out of concern for their children. One Single Parent, who had her child out of wedlock and is no longer in a relationship with the child's father mentioned that she is cautious – as any parent should be as to who she exposes her young daughter to; and the fact that she has a young daughter has been the primary reason for her not dating more frequently. Another Single Parent who is a divorcee cited concern for her two children as well as the reason that she did not date when they were younger; her children are now teenagers and she has been dating someone for a number of months. This single mom stated that she wanted to be sure of this man's character and integrity before introducing him to her children. The commonality from the single mothers I surveyed was that their children were their primary focus and concern and if this meant that they would not date while the children were young, so be it.

Regardless of what any of the cited studies may suggest or what society says, the Single Parent must hold fast to the word of God standing firm in knowing that knowledge and wisdom in raising your children and deciding to marry will come from God; and that as a Single Parent you will have everything that you need to raise a healthy, whole human being who will be a contributing member of society.

Pitfall: The Single Parent must be careful to not

make her children her life. Because her children will grow up and begin to live a life of their own. My research indicated that most single mothers sacrifice themselves for their children. The Single Parent must first of all know who she is independent of her children and not lose sight of self while she raises her children. Some women will choose to be single until they raise their children, others may desire a mate who will help them parent, and then there are those who, like one of the widows, will desire to remain single; the right choice concerning marriage as a single parent is up to each individual. What is right for one person may not be right for someone else.

Blending a family has challenges of its own and should not be entered into lightly. The Single Parent should be in much prayer seeking direction from God concerning the decision to marry or remain single.

CHAPTER 6

THE CHURCH SISTER

The infamous Church Sister—all the Saints know her. She is the lady at church who, when asked if she is dating will say, "I'm dating Jesus" or "Jesus is all the man I need." You got to love the Church Sister. Like other single ladies, she has her list of all the characteristics her future husband must have. She is at the church morning, noon, and night on Sundays and several times during the week for choir rehearsal, dance practice, women's meeting, Bible study, and any other church-related event or service – her motto, "a girl can never get too much Word." And in general, she is quite faithful to the ministry.

The most positive attribute of the Church Sister's personality is that she has busied herself to the point where she has no time to negatively contemplate her single state of being. For most women like this, it simply is a non-issue for them. They are quite content in the season that they are in—since they are dating "Jesus."

This personality can sometimes be viewed as being very radical in the dating scene; my theory of the "I'm dating Jesus" attitude comes from a woman's desire to not be hurt in a relationship and is her defense mechanism. This attitude exudes the aura, "if you want to date me, you must come correct – I have no time for dating games." A major downfall of this personality is that this lady can have unrealistic expectations for her future mate.

The Church Sister was definitely me when I was single. I was actually a Church Sister with a little bit of the Professional Student swirled in. When I made my commitment to prepare myself for my mate, I was in graduate school working on a master's degree, had made plans to attend law school, and was just beginning my career in professional sports administration. I was happy, content, and on my way to becoming a sports and entertainment attorney. As far as my dating life, I was one of the Church Sisters who would say, "right now it's me and Jesus and that's enough!"

During this time, I was at my church constantly during the week: on Sundays for church and Sunday school, on Tuesdays for women's fellowship, on Wednesdays for Bible study and on Saturdays for dance ministry practices. Sometimes I felt as if I was married to my church since I spent so much time there. Being that I was single and had no children, my commitment to the church was in part my way of serving selflessly for I knew that when I was married and had children my priorities would shift. This was also part of my growth process. My time at the various services at my church allowed me to bond with and learn from seasoned women who were married, get to know and network with other single sisters, and build up myself spiritually.

The Church Sister who desires to be married is almost there. She is one step away from being a Lady-in-Waiting; however, she must first realize that the "it's me and Jesus" or the "I'm dating Jesus" attitude is impossible to maintain. Having Christ as the head of her life is very much in order and in line with God's word, however going as far as substituting her relationship with Christ for a mate will eventually backfire. Woman was made for man, and the word of God says, "He who finds a wife finds what is good and receives favor from the LORD" (Proverbs 18:22 NIV). And not just the Church Sister, but every single woman who desires to be married should focus on becoming the best person that she can be for herself and her future husband. The Church Sister should use her season of singleness to become the whole individual who will need to enter into marriage with another person. Marriage is a constant act of service and sacrifice – and there are many who struggle with this; if there is a selfish bone in the Church Sister's body, this is the time to deal with that issue.

Oftentimes the Church Sister, like me during my season of singleness, has insecurities that she must deal with. For me, I was exposed to divorce at an early age. My parents separated when I was four years old, my maternal grandparents divorced shortly after, then during the course of my teen and young adult years, I witnessed many of my aunts and uncles divorce. By the time I came of age, I had such a negative view of marriage that I personally felt my destiny was to marry then divorce. Thus, my "it's me and Jesus attitude" was born. I felt like Jesus would never leave me, lie to me, cheat on me, or beat me. I was quite happy for a time during my season of singleness with this attitude.

Pitfall: The major issue with the Church Sister is that spiritually, you can say "it's me and Jesus" or that "you are dating Jesus," but in the natural, let's be real. Deep down inside we both know that you really desire a mate. I get the concept of the "I'm dating Jesus" stance. Much of which is born from not wanting to be hurt and disappointed by another man. I understand the Church Sister, because I was the Church Sister. Just as we are human and make mistakes and are the source of disappointment, realize that there is no man who will be the perfect Jesus who walked this earth and walked on water. The most stellar of a Christian man will at some point, disappoint you. That's life. People in our lives disappoint us by not measuring up to a particular standard or expectation. Simply realize that they are not Jesus – they are not perfect and neither are you. Accept your future husband for who he is—his shortcomings and all—and love him regardless of his faults and imperfections, knowing that you are not perfect either.

An additional word of caution to the Church Sister is to NOT fall for the counterfeit. The counterfeit mate is a man who appears to be the man for you when he is really a fake and not what he appears to be. Before I was engaged to my husband, I was engaged to a guy that I dated in college. We dated on and off for a number of years and attempted to make a long distance relationship work when I was into year two of my process of preparation. During this time, I was especially weak because my mom was gravely ill and I lived more than 1,500 miles away in another state. I was under a tremendous amount of stress trying to cope with a terminally ill mother and felt as though my guard was down. I ran into familiar arms when we started dating again and was blind to the fact that a long distance relationship simply would not work for us since we had tried and failed once before.

I have met many Christian ladies who, like me, were either engaged to a counterfeit or for others, married to a counterfeit; I therefore devoted an entire chapter to this trap of the enemy.

CHAPTER 7

RUNAWAY BRIDE

Oh me, oh my, she's always in a quandary and never seems to know quite what to do. She's been engaged more than once but has never seen the engagement through. If you've never been married and have been engaged more than once, this could be you.

Do you know her, the perpetual fiancée? She always has a beautiful diamond engagement ring but has not made her way down the aisle. She has a "list" that consists of no less than 30 characteristics that her ideal mate must meet, such as good credit, nice car, good job, home owner, etc., etc. Most of her list will consist of material things that she probably hasn't obtained herself. She will not compromise because she has waited too long for "Mr. Right" to settle for "Mr. Wrong."

Of the single lady surveys that I administered and received back, no one categorized themselves as a Runaway Bride even if they had been engaged more than once. I don't believe that any woman who has been engaged and never married would want to be categorized as a Runaway Bride since there are such negative connotations attached to this title. Most of us think of the Runaway Bride as the confused bride-to-be who disappears on the morning of her wedding and leaves the groom at the altar. We think of the runaway brides we have heard about on the news and describe her as a flake. For the purpose of this book, the Runaway Bride is a single lady who has been engaged more than once, but never married.

I recall a time when I was in the company of a couple of runaway brides. There was a group of us single ladies out on the town for a ladies night. We were all talking, sharing, and having a good time as us girls do when we are together. At some point in the conversation we started discussing fiancés, engagements, and marriage. I was one in the group who had never been married or engaged and was quite surprised at how casually two ladies in the group spoke of their engagement process, including how callously the engagements were called off. To me, both ladies spoke as if, "getting the ring" was a game to them and they had somehow won. My initial thought was, "wow, so it's that easy for some people." However, for the lady who understands what an engagement means, her outlook is totally different.

An engagement is a promise to marry and should not be taken lightly. The engagement ring in

Western culture is a betrothal gift to the woman after she accepts the marriage proposal and signifies a formal agreement for a future marriage. The practice of engagement has a long history in society and dates back to biblical times; one such example, when Mary – the mother of Jesus was betrothed to Joseph (Matthew 1:18-24 NKJV). During this time, the betrothal was arranged by the fathers and was quite different and of a more serious nature than our current day Western engagement period. Scripture tells us that Joseph considered divorcing Mary when he found out that she was pregnant during their betrothal period; this to preserve his honor. Jewish customs and law demanded that a man divorce his wife for adultery; failure to do so would mean that his house would be a disgrace and he would be viewed as one who was harboring a prostitute. However, divine intervention convinced Joseph not to divorce Mary and he took her in as his wife. We further read in scripture that Joseph and Mary did not consummate their marriage until after the birth of Jesus.

The story of Joseph and Mary's betrothal is a beautiful example of trusting God and honoring a vow. Joseph not only took Mary in as his wife, but respected her and did not have sexual relations until after she had given birth. Is it because we live in a society where our word is no longer our bond that the Runaway Bride views their engagement as something trivial?

Pitfall: Based on my observation of the Runaway Bride personality in the ladies that I personally observed, I conclude that deep down inside, one of the Runaway Brides whom I will call Jane has a void, an emptiness that prevents her from following through on her promise to marry. And the other, I will call Janine. She has an issue with commitment.

My reason for making the assertion that Jane has a void that prevents her from going through with her engagements is that she clearly has no problem attracting a man and getting engaged. However, actually following through on the promise to marry is lacking. Jane was the Runaway Bride who spoke very cavalierly about being engaged three times. She did not give details as to why each of her engagements was called off. She simply laughed and shrugged at the fact that she had been previously engaged, but never married and each time kept the rings. I found her to be cold and calculating; seemed as if the men in her past cared more about her than she did for them. There appeared to be a void in her life – a void that is too much for a man to fill – one that God alone can fill.

If you see yourself in Jane or your situation being parallel to hers, I suggest you back away from dating and any further engagements for a minute and spend some quality time with yourself and God. Seek the Master's face and ask Him to reveal where you are lacking and what is preventing you from moving forward with marriage. Sometimes the hardest thing to do is admit that we have a fault. When we face our idiosyncrasies and deal with our negative attributes, those qualities about us that are viewed as shortcomings, we come away better than we were before and are on our way to being a whole individual capable of selflessly giving of ourselves.

Janine is the Runaway Bride who appeared to

have an issue with commitment. She discussed having been engaged, was in the process of planning her wedding – then got cold feet. She did not elaborate on any particular issue that caused her to have a change of heart, other than moving forward with the wedding and marriage plans did not feel right with this particular guy. She also discussed another serious relationship where they discussed marriage and were engaged but she did not have a ring. This relationship did not work out either.

Janine must first do some soul searching and find out who she really is so that she will know what she really wants—and more importantly—needs in a mate; she must determine what is important to her. In her current state of mind, my conclusion is that she has an unrealistic or unhealthy expectation of what marriage really is. The closer she came to making the commitment to marriage she realized that marriage was not something that she wanted at that time in her life with either guy.

Both of these Runaway Brides must do some deep soul searching to nail down and deal with whatever issues they are dealing with concerning marriage. Sometimes issues that we face may not be apparent to us on the surface. I therefore suggest that these ladies or anyone else who sees herself in one of the previous examples, strongly consider Christian counseling to deal with deep-seated issues concerning marriage and/or commitment.

CHAPTER 8

LADY-IN-WAITING

The Lady-in-Waiting is the single lady who is engaged to be married. Once engaged, I was the Lady-in-Waiting. After one failed engagement, I was finally where I had longed to be — on my way down the aisle. The man who would one day be my husband and I began going out in May, became engaged in December and got married in April — twelve months encompassed our courtship, dating, and engagement period. A lot of women ask me, "How did you know he was THE ONE? You guys dated and got married all in a year." My response is one that the single woman never likes to hear, "I just knew."

When I was single, I often asked married women the same question, "How did you know that your husband was the one?" They all answered the same, "Terry, I just knew that he was the one." This may be hard to accept for the single woman, but trust me, when a man is the right one for you, you will know it. There will be a peace about him in your spirit. I cannot explain it — you just feel it. A wise person once said, "Do not marry someone who you are madly in love with — because people now-a-days fall out of love. Marry someone who you want to grow old with."

Prior to becoming engaged, if you have completely prepared yourself for the next level — that is engagement and marriage — knowing who your mate is will not be as ceremonial as you think. Things will simply fall into place. If you are having major issues in a relationship prior to marriage, this is a major red flag and you should pump the brakes and reassess the situation. By all means do not overlook the small things, either. If there is something about a man that really irritates you or if it is something that you feel you cannot live with and you are thinking that you will change him once you are married — this as well is a red flag — proceed with caution.

The Lady-in-Waiting is where many single ladies desire to be, especially those who feel that they are "ready" for marriage. I strongly suggest that these singles ladies use their season of singleness to focus on self. Once you are married, marriage is all about the other person, your spouse. If you are thinking that marriage will be all about you, you are sadly mistaken and are in for a rude awakening. Marriage is a constant act of selfless service. You are constantly giving to the other person, not because you want something out of it, but because you realize a wife's place in marriage and that is to be a help meet to her husband. I once read somewhere that God did not take a bone from Adam's skull to frame Eve because it is not the wife's place to have rule over her husband; neither did He take a bone from Adam's feet because Adam is to not walk over his wife; but He took a bone from Adam's rib, illustrating that the wife is to stand side by side with her husband supporting him – submitting to him who is submitted to Christ. (Genesis 2:20-24 NIV). And in turn the husband is commanded to love his wife as Christ loved the church and gave himself for it (Ephesians 5:25 NKJV).

The Lady-in-Waiting v. The Runaway Bride

The Lady-in-Waiting and Runaway Bride may seem as if they are the same personality because they are both engaged to be married. However, they are quite different. Their mindset and outlook of what it means to be engaged is like night and day; the two personalities are distinguished by not just their understanding of what it means to be engaged but by their commitment to the engagement.

The Lady-in-Waiting knows exactly what it means to be engaged to be married; she knows the importance of this phase in the process of marriage. Her engagement is not trivial nor is it a game about getting a ring. The Lady-in-Waiting has prepared herself for her mate. This season has come through much patience, prayer, and fasting. She has no problem following through on her promise to marry. In fact, she looks forward to her wedding day with great anticipation.

In contrast, the Runaway Bride has a twisted

view of her engagement and impending marriage. Instead of looking forward to her wedding day, she is typically contemplating a way out of the engagement. The Runaway Brides I encountered and discussed in the Runaway Bride chapter have a variety of issues going on: 1) fear of long-term commitment, 2) inability to follow through with a serious promise and 3) lack of mutual love for the other person. This puts the Runaway Bride at the opposite end of the spectrum in comparison to the Lady-in-Waiting.

Pitfall: My only word of caution to the Lady-in-Waiting is to not misplace her priorities, by busying herself to the point where she stops doing those things that got her to this blessed state. I have witnessed many engaged ladies twist their priorities as a result of being engaged. In the excitement of planning their wedding, they are so busy feeding their soul realm that they neglect their spirit.

These ladies are shopping for dresses, looking at wedding halls, interviewing wedding planners, choosing bridesmaids, going over menu choices, and ordering invitations while constantly revising the guest list and trying to decide on a honeymoon destination. In other words, the Lady-in-Waiting is insanely consumed with her wedding plans at this point in her life. She has no time to pray, and going to church on the regular is simply out of the question, since some of her best wedding details are taken care of on Sundays. She constantly says, "God knows my heart." Too often, this bride-to-be has busied herself preparing for the dream wedding day she has always wanted that she forgets that there will be a marriage after the wedding, and this will require perpetual nourishment.

While the details of the Lady-in-Waiting's wedding fulfill her soul realm which is her mind, will, and emotions – it is important that she does not neglect her spirit man, which is the core of her being and how she relates to God. Her spirit man is nourished when she attends church, Bible study, and maintains her prayer life. Humans are tri-part beings: we are a spirit being living in a body and possessing a soul. The person inside of us is our spirit – our born-again nature; our soul is not born again. Being that our spirit and soul are constantly battling each other, the Lady-in-Waiting must not allow her soul realm to overpower her spirit being.

My advice to the Lady-in-Waiting is to enjoy your engagement and wedding planning to the fullest, but remember that you are *a bride for a day – a wife for a lifetime.* During this time of wedding day preparations, continue building up yourself for your mate. Don't stop doing those things that made you attractive to your soon to be husband. Continue with your prayer life, continue attending your place of worship, and, finally, continue your physical upkeep. I have heard of and witnessed women who have "let themselves go" because they now have a man. This is not fair. Whatever you were doing prior to meeting your fiancé and future husband, you should continue doing during your engagement and especially during your marriage. It is imperative that you prepare yourself to be a wife. In closing, remember that you are striving to be a bride for a day—a wife for a lifetime.

PART II: ALWAYS A BRIDESMAID

CHAPTER 9

ALWAYS A BRIDESMAID

We've all heard the clichés, "Always a Bridesmaid ~ Never a Bride!" or "The Leading Lady and the Best Friend" and perhaps the most well-known of them all, the "Hero and the Sidekick." About five years into my seven-year journey, on any particular day either of those descriptions summed up exactly how I felt. During this time, I was going through a difficult break-up with my first fiancé, I was taking night classes in an eleven-month program to get a professional certification, and I had also started a new job in a different industry. To say that I was stressed out is a marginalization of my situation. In the midst of everything going on in my personal and professional life, several of my friends, acquaintances, and co-workers were getting married. I felt as if everyone around me was either married or engaged to be married. The circle of single ladies that once surrounded me was becoming smaller by the year.

Instead of the feeling of excitement and anticipation that I felt when I began my journey, I started to feel like I was drowning in a sea of hopelessness as I strived to grow and be a better person with the hope of one day being a wife.

Will You Be a Bridesmaid in My Wedding?

I remember the first phone call from one of my good friends from college. After a long day at work, I returned a missed call from her. We exchanged courtesies then she told me how she appreciated my support and words of encouragement when she was going through a difficult time in her relationship and that they had worked through their issues and she was planning her wedding. Then excitedly asked me, "Will you be a bridesmaid in my wedding?"

I answered, "Yes, of course! I will be honored to stand with you."

I was elated that my friend was about to be married to the love of her life. In the back of my mind I was wondering, "Lord when will it be my time?"

This scenario played out several more times before I became the bride. Each time a friend called me and asked if I would be in their wedding my heart was always overjoyed for my friend and sad for me, because I sometimes felt as if God had forgotten that I too desired a husband.

Regardless of how hopeless I felt about my own situation, I always rose to the occasion for my friends. I did not want to be the source of any stress for my friends – most brides are under a tremendous amount of pressure, and I felt my duty as a friend and bridesmaid was to be as amicable as possible during the wedding experience. I have observed some women selfishly sabotage their friend's wedding experience because they were jealous. I've witnessed actions such as close friends refusing to be in their friend's wedding for trivial reasons, friends who have agreed to be in the wedding only to back out at various stages in the process for one reason or another, and the classic one – friends who have agreed to be in the wedding that whine, moan, and complain the entire time. I've seen the bridesmaids who hate the dress and/or feel like it is too expensive, don't like the shoes, complain about the jewelry, regardless of what the bride-to-be does. They are never satisfied. This was never me.

In my heart I longed to be the bride, however, I never allowed my personal desire to fester to the point where I was jealous of one of my friends. I knew that being jealous of what God was doing in their life was counterproductive to where I knew God was taking me. I always felt like this is not my time, but I will have my time so there is no need to be envious or jealous – celebrate their occasion.

The Single Best Friend with All the Advice

During my season of singleness, I somehow became the friend with all the relationship advice. I really don't know how this came to be. I just realized at some point during my preparation process that a lot of my friends were calling me with their relationship issues and asking for advice. My friends have always told me that I am like the "mom" of the group. This perhaps is why many of them sought me for relationship advice. I, however, felt like I was blind and I was leading the blind. Initially, I freely gave advice to any and all of my friends who called. My giving advice also happened while I was engaged to my first fiancé and was having my own relationship issues to contend with. After hearing several comedians jokingly refer to their girlfriend or wife's "single best friend with all the advice" I had an aha moment! I realized that I had all the answers for everyone else, but in my own situation I was struggling with my own advice concerning what I should do.

In my heart, I knew exactly what I needed to do regarding my engagement – but knowing what to do and doing it are distinctively different. I had a major struggle internally with my decision. The struggle was so intense that it took me months to actually end my engagement. In my mind I was no longer engaged long before I officially called the engagement off. I became so frustrated with myself that I stopped giving relationship advice to my friends. I had one friend who was extra persistent in wanting advice about her situation that I finally told her to stop asking me for advice because I have relationship issues of my own. I jokingly, but seriously, told her that I am no longer your single friend with all the advice! And that I would no longer feel a little heated and convicted when I heard a comedian refer to his girlfriend or wife's "single best friend with all the advice."

CHAPTER 10

THE INFAMOUS LIST

What exactly is "the Infamous List?" I believe that most, if not all, of the single women I have ever known have a list of qualities that they desire in a mate. This list can be mental or more commonly is physical – an actual list that is written or typed and identifies qualities such as: he must be a Christian, honest, trustworthy, loyal, handsome, hardworking, athletic, at least 6 feet tall, well-groomed, compassionate, articulate, funny. The list goes on and on and on... You get the idea. And yes, I had a list as well.

I personally feel that there is nothing wrong with a woman having a list of qualities that she desires in a mate. When I was single, I had a mental list of the things that I desired in a mate. After attending an event for single Christians, I remember the speaker encouraging us singles to write down what we desired in a mate. I complied and my list started out as a handwritten list on a yellow sticky note. As I became more discerning about what I desired, my list grew. I remember attaching the sticky note to a piece of personal stationery and continuing the list to the point where I used up one side of the stationery and had started on the back side of the paper. As my list continued to grow, I finally typed the list, printed it – then ceremoniously prayed over the list and put the folded paper in my Bible on the same page as one of my favorite verses as a single, Matthew 6:33 (NKJV), "But seek first the kingdom of God and his righteousness, and all these things shall be added to you," as I was believing God for a great and mighty man of God. I remember being so proud of my list. At that time, I was not concerned with whether or not this scripture was even appropriate in my situation and me believing God for a husband. I just knew that the Word spoke to me in this scripture and said, "Make God your first priority in life and God will add things to your life – do not seek things, seek the righteousness of God and He will give you the things that your heart desires." I held this close to my heart for years as a single because my journey was seven years. And during those seven years I was tempted to help God out a little in picking out a mate for myself. During those years, there were several eligible men that I was interested in – I now realize that God had something greater in store for me. I just needed to be patient.

My making the commitment to prepare myself to become a wife and actually becoming a wife did not happen overnight. God's plan was quite different from mine. When I started my journey I just knew that I would be ready for a husband in six months to a year. However, at the end of one year, I had no idea that I had just begun the journey. My list was a continuous work in progress during the first three to four years; after which time, the list was placed in my Bible.

As a single Christian believing God for a husband, it is so easy to become frustrated and want to give up when you are waiting for the promise to manifest and it does not happen within the time that you think it should. I know because I have been there. The Word of God says that hope deferred makes the heart sick (Proverbs 13:12a NKJV). In this scripture, the word sick means to be ill, weak, to become faint. I have been at a place where my heart was sick because I longed to be someone's wife. During difficult times in my journey, I always found renewed hope and strength in the Word of God. The scripture ends with, "But when the desire comes, it is a tree of life." In other words, when the thing that we long for manifests or happens this brings a renewed hope or vigor to our lives.

I caution against allowing the times when you are frustrated along the way or you are low in faith about a husband to spur you to dismiss or compromise on your list. Do not lower your standards and do not start doing things that are counterproductive to your progress. The Word says, "My brethren, count it all joy when you fall into various trials, knowing that the testing of your faith produces patience. But let patience have its perfect work, that you may be perfect and complete, lacking nothing" (James 1:2-4 NKJV). The key to success during a difficult season is patience. Allow God to work out in you and do whatever He needs to do to make you a bride that a Godly man would be honored to have.

Wants and Desires v. Must-Haves

I do not want to confuse compromising your standard as it relates to your list and differentiating your wants and desires from your must-haves with each other. At some point, every list should be reviewed and purged, categorizing the wants and desires from the must-haves, which are things that you need and are not willing to compromise on.

Wants and desires versus must-haves, almost sounds like an exotic wrestling match. And in many ways, it is. Those things that we want and desire in a mate versus those things that we must have may battle with each other from time to time regarding their priority. Those things that a single lady may want or desire are the things that she feels a need, desire, a craving, or longing for. Those things that are must-haves are things that she needs. Her potential mate absolutely must possess these characteristics to even be in the running or to be considered as husband material.

Wants and desires on a list may be things such as physical characteristics and certain personality traits, vocation, and political preference. Wants and desires must not be confused with must-haves. For example, a single lady may desire a mate who is at least 6' tall. If she meets a man who is 5'10" will she not consider him because of his height even if he meets other characteristics on her list? Height is a physical characteristic and certainly should not be a deal breaker. Or what if one of your desires is that he be funny, but you meet a man who has a dry sense of humor or he does not have a funny personality at all. Sense of humor is a personality trait that I hope would not be a deal breaker. On the contrary, negative personality traits such as arrogance, callousness, or laziness are personality traits that could very well be deal breakers. The physical characteristics area of your list should be carefully reviewed and purged. Physical characteristics are vain and really should not be a deal breaker. There is nothing wrong with desiring a tall, athletic man with nice teeth – but, assess the population, or the pool of men available. If you are a single lady in your thirties or forties, you may be disappointed when you realize that the available men in your age group may not be as athletically built as you would like. This should not be a deal breaker; weight can be managed with lifestyle changes. A flawed personality may prove to be more difficult to deal with in the long-run. Personality traits should always take priority over physical characteristics. Would you rather have a man who is a hard worker, nice, honest, and he adores you but is a little over weight or a man who is in tip-top shape, a little flirty, talks down to you, and is a liar? Let's be clear, when it comes to wants and desires, your ordained husband may not meet every single one of those characteristics on your list. This should not be a disappointment, but a mature realization. The goal is for God to bless your spirit, not your flesh.

Must-haves are characteristics that are deal breakers such as: faith or belief in Christ, critical personality traits, stance on child rearing and/or the desire to have children and career goals and aspirations.

Being of the same faith is important in a

marriage. If you are a Christian, my guess is that you would like to marry a Christian. Religious beliefs and practices are important in our everyday lives and having someone who is of like faith can definitely be considered a must-have. Same as ideals on child rearing; some women may prefer an authoritative type as a father to their children. Others may despise this type of child rearing and may prefer someone who is more an authoritarian or maybe even permissive in their disciplining style. This can definitely be a deal breaker. Imagine the issues a couple would have if they have very different views on what is appropriate child rearing.

As you evaluate your list, whether or not the person wants children or if you already have children, whether or not the person is accepting of children that you already have is important. Just as there are some people who do not want children, there are some people who do not want to marry someone who already has children – they have no desire to be a stepparent. This would obviously be a deal breaker.

I have heard of ladies who have tried to keep their child or children from a previous relationship a secret as they are getting to know someone. I personally think this is a deceitful tactic – as if the lady is trying to ensure that the guy is taking a liking to her, and then she divulges that she has a child or children. If you have a child or children this should be made known early on in the courtship. Letting someone know that you are a parent is a critical piece of information that should be shared without reservation; however, introducing them to your child should not happen until you are sure this is someone you are planning to move forward in a relationship with and trust to bring them into your child's life. Therefore, a person's feelings about children that are not his own is a definite factor. If the man you are dating or considering marrying has negative feelings or ideas about being with someone who has children, this is a deal breaker. Do not compromise here.

As a single woman, to have a list is important. And you want to be clear about what you desire and what you must have in a mate. Be realistic about your expectations, but never compromise when it comes to your list.

CHAPTER 11

GETTING TO THE LADY-IN-WAITING

I received the book, *Knight in Shining Armor* from one of my cousins, Paula. She was so blessed after reading this book that she purchased a copy for me and suggested I read it as well. I strongly suggest that any single woman desiring to be married read this book by author P.B. Wilson. Shortly after I finished reading the book, I was so inspired by the words of wisdom shared by Mrs. Wilson that I made a commitment to begin preparing myself for a husband and mate; this was January 20, 1998. When I made this commitment, I did not realize that the full process for me would span more than seven years. I was married on April 2, 2005. From January 20, 1998 until April 2, 2005—just over seven years—was my season of preparation.

A lot happened in my life during those seven years of preparation: I began to fervently pursue my purpose in life, completed my master's degree, diverted my career path, travelled to Maui, Hawaii, on vacation, became engaged—then unengaged. The biggest of all was that my Mom passed away, and overnight I became a single parent by taking in my 12-year-old brother.

I went from being a single, happy-go-lucky, career-minded, twenty-something-year-old woman, to being a single parent concerned with what neighborhood I should buy a house, what school district had the best schools for my brother, what would my brother do for funding for his college education, and most importantly—how would I teach this boy to become a man. I soon became overwhelmed with life.

We Plan ~ God Laughs

Several months after my mother passed away, as I settled into my new life of single parenthood, I decided to leave my career in professional sports and entertainment and pursue a career path that would allow me to work more traditional hours so that I could spend more time with my brother. This was a hard decision for me, since I had been planning and preparing for a career in the entertainment industry—and more specifically sports entertainment—since obtaining my undergraduate degree. At no time did I ever dream that I would be a single parent having to make the type of decisions I was forced to make at that point in my life. After brief employment with a nonprofit, I decided to start a new career track in the field of Paralegal Studies, thinking that if I ever made a final decision to go to law school, experience as a paralegal would provide an excellent foundation for me as an attorney.

Over the next few years, my time as a paralegal

allowed me to make a great wage and have good benefits for my brother and myself. I was able to work traditional hours, which allowed me to be home in the evening, nights, and weekends to spend quality time with him. I have often contemplated my decision to leave my career in sports and entertainment and have wondered, "Where would that career path have taken me?" Although I sometimes look back, I never regret doing what I felt was best for my brother and me at that time in my life. By being still and allowing God to work in my life, I know that I was in the proper place to be blessed with my husband.

CHAPTER 12

SINGLE FOR A SEASON

My Work in the Ministry

I heard a wise person say, "While you are single put your hands to the plow and do something." While preparing for my husband, I faithfully served in my church. During this season in my process, I was definitely the Church Sister. I attended Pilgrim Rest Baptist Church in Phoenix, Arizona – which has one of the largest African American congregations in Phoenix. During this time the church was experiencing a tremendous amount of growth, and had just completed construction on and paid for a multi-million dollar worship edifice. The church was starting phase two of a three-phase building project. The congregation was an eclectic mix of working and middle class parishioners with its share of wealthy church goers that included prominent business owners, corporate executives, and professional athletes. So to say that there was a nice selection of men is an understatement.

I used the "extra time" that I had while I was single to serve young ladies at my church as the dance ministry leader. I volunteered two Saturdays out of every month and worked with a group of children and youth at my church teaching and rehearsing liturgical dance. What started out as a group of four to six kids in the beginning, grew to be more than 50 praise dancers and a leadership team that included myself and three other ladies by the time I resigned from the ministry. My motivation to serve while I was single came in me knowing that when I married, my time and devotion would be to my husband. I, therefore, used my season of singleness to pour into young people's lives as so many had poured into my life when I was a youth.

I encourage single ladies to use their time as a single wisely by pursuing and finding their passion prior to marriage. Never enter into a marriage without a clear vision of who you are and what you aspire to be and do in life. I am passionate about helping and giving back to young people in the community and church. So volunteering in the youth ministry for me is natural. Being the oldest of five children and being a part of such a large family, I never viewed myself as the type that liked to work with kids – through my willingness to volunteer and try new things, I learned that I really enjoy volunteering for causes that benefit young people.

I volunteered in the youth ministry at my church for six years before I married. Approximately, 3 ½ years in, I met with the youth pastor and told him that I felt strongly in my spirit that I only had about another year and a half with the dance ministry because I felt that the Lord was leading me in a new direction. And that he should start thinking about a successor for the dance ministry once I was done. When I had this discussion with the youth pastor, in my mind the new direction that I was thinking was law school. God obviously had other plans.

Hope Deferred Makes the Heart Sick

In life, we prepare for all sorts of things: we prepare for a career by going to school; while in school we prepare for exams by studying; and once we are in the workplace, we prepare for a promotion by learning the job duties or skills needed for the next level. During your season of singleness, begin preparing for your God-ordained husband. Your process of preparation will be different from mine because we are different people and at varying levels in our walk with Christ. Later in the book, I discuss in detail my process.

If your season of preparation spans years as mine did, I want to encourage you to not get tired, don't quit, and don't give in to temptation and compromise on what you are believing God for. Continue pressing toward that which you have prayed for and are believing and waiting on God for. As the saying goes, "When **opportunity** meets **preparation**, it equals **success**."

At the time, I did not know it, but I was approaching the end of my preparation process. On this particular evening, I was feeling a little overwhelmed and frustrated with my situation. I was just over a year removed from ending my engagement, and I was also facing surmounting debt from a business that I had started. I decided to attend an event at my cousin Paula's church where a travelling minister would be ministering in the prophetic realm. When she offered me the invitation to attend, I was initially hesitant because I normally do not attend religious events where I do not know or have not heard of the person ministering the Word. I remember thinking, "What the heck, this is a Sunday evening, I have no plans – it can't hurt to go, listen, and observe." Before I left my house I uttered a prayer that if this lady was a false prophet I asked God to cause her to overlook me in the crowd, but if she was a true prophet of God, I was open to receive.

This is what the minister said as she ministered among the crowd of attendees:

"Every person that's in this room tonight under the sound of my voice, I have prayed for you. I have prayed for you. And I asked the Lord to call those people that He wanted to bring and to use unusual methods do whatever He wants. You were one that God wanted to bring to this place. And God has a blessing for you before you leave. God has a rich blessing. "

The following is what she said to me:

"This sister right here ... [prays in tongues] There's the presence of God in this place [raise your hands] [prays in tongues] woman of God, that's an intercessor that has been before God hallelujah [prays in tongues] and He says to look not upon the circumstance, hallelujah, cause the eye has cast down,

and He says sister daughter do not be downcast for I want you to know that the Lord is saying to the downtrodden that I'm going to pull you up and tonight the spirit of the Lord is reaching in and He's pulling you up and that which hope deferred has made the heart sick it seems like you looked and you've looked and you're standing for a miracle but I want you to know that God is coming through, hallelujah. You're beautifully dressed but I want you to know there's a financial break through that you need in your life that God is going to place through but right now more than anything honey what He wants to do is wrap you up and He wants to do an impartation into your spirit into your spirit into your spirit and He's saying come on up come on up come on up and the thing that which has tried to hold you back tonight come up and there it is there it is in Jesus name now receive hallelujah healing in the name of Jesus hallelujah hallelujah. Anointing, there it is. Anointing an increase of anointing increase more of you Jesus more of you Jesus more of you Jesus hallelujah more of you Jesus more of you Lord more of you Lord more of you Lord. ..."

After she was done speaking to me, my cousin Paula came up to me, hugged me and put an offering in my hand and told me to seal that Word with an offering. At that moment, I wasn't concerned with the amount I simply took the money and put it in the offering basket. Whatever the amount, I was truly grateful for it, because I had absolutely no money at that moment to put into an offering. And in my heart I really wanted to give an offering.

The minister's words were on point, and very

relevant to my situation. When the Prophet stated that "hope deferred makes the heart sick" I felt as if I would faint, because that scripture summed up how I felt at that moment. At this point in my process, although content, I was discouraged. She also addressed my financial situation. She stated that I was in need of a financial break through – this was an understatement. I felt like I was in need of a financial miracle. My sales had tapered off in the business that I had started, and I could not keep up with my payments to my creditors in addition to my personal expenses every month. When faced with which bills I would pay – business or personal, I chose to pay my personal expenses; which meant that my business creditors were demanding payments from me.

As I left the church building, I had no doubt in my mind that this was a Word directly from God. The minister struck down any doubt I may have had when she told us that she had prayed for all of us and asked God to send the people there He wanted to be in attendance. This for me was confirmation that she was a messenger sent by God. I listened to the cassette tape that contained the prophetic words that she had spoken that evening over and over on the drive home; and continued to listen to the tape in the weeks to come. I have a hard time explaining how comforting and timely her words were for me. That prophetic word came at a time in my process when I desperately needed encouragement to keep waiting and believing God for my husband. This word energized me to keep pressing forward.

Regarding my finances, I was hoping for a

financial miracle. I did not receive a miracle, but my financial breakthrough did come a few months later. I initially made payment arrangements with my creditors and ultimately refinanced my townhouse – pulled money out and paid the remaining debts in full. And in the midst of budget cuts at my job, I received a pay increase.

CHAPTER 13

BRIDE FOR A DAY ~ WIFE FOR A LIFETIME

Despite the major life changes I experienced during my season of preparation—losing my mother, becoming a parent to my younger brother, changing careers, and getting engaged then subsequently calling off the engagement—I maintained my commitment to continue preparing myself for a husband, and more importantly, the husband God had ordained for me.

I used the time that I was single to prepare myself to not only be a bride, but to be a wife. I maintained my commitment of preparing myself to be a wife because I was of the mindset that I would be a bride for a day — a wife for a lifetime. I continually reminded myself, especially once I became engaged and actually started preparing for my wedding day, that I would not lose sight of what got me to this point, but to continue preparing, to continue praying, and to continue seeking God for guidance. I was determined not to fall into the trap of being the misguided Lady-in-Waiting, who is so consumed with her wedding that she forgets about or stops doing those things that got her to that point.

Once a woman becomes engaged to be married it is so easy to lose focus and become sidetracked with the details of preparing for her big wedding day. I caution against this. As I discussed in the "Lady-in-Waiting" chapter of this book, which is specifically targeted toward those women who are engaged to be married and are actively planning their weddings, continue doing those things that got you to the point of being a Lady-in-Waiting or bride-to-be. Don't stop going to church because you are too busy; don't slack off of your prayer time because you are too tired; and don't stop reading your Bible. Now more than ever, you need to be spending quality time with God because once you are married, your primary focus will be your husband.

Adorned In Holiness

As women, we spend unspeakable amounts of money to make ourselves pretty on the outside. We invest in our hair and nails; we get massages, buy gym memberships, clothes and shoes all to look good. And nothing is wrong with beautifying the outside of our body. On the contrary, how much do we invest to beautify our inside? As you prepare to become a wife, do not neglect your innermost well-being. Remember the daily battle between your spirit and your soul.

The word says, "Charm is deceitful and beauty is passing, but a woman who fears the Lord, she shall be praised." (Proverbs 31:30 NKJV) How often have you heard a husband (or wife) say that when they met their spouse they were one way, and now that they know their spouse, they are different? This drives home the point that charm is deceitful. Our charm is our ability to attract or please others through our personality. And we have been taught that first impressions are lasting impressions; and we should always make a good first impression. For example, when a couple is dating, both people will obviously show their best selves at all times in the beginning – each wanting to impress the other. Then once the couple is married, their true natures eventually begin to surface. For some couples, the other person's true nature begins to show during the engagement period. And as long as a person's true nature is not too far from their first impression, most couples move past this revelation. Ladies do not be seduced by a man's ability to charm. And vice versa: Do not think that you will be able to attract and keep a man based on your ability to charm him. Your true nature will always come through. Therefore, spend time working on your character and you will not have to resort to deceptive tactics to attract a man.

The next part of the scripture says that "beauty is passing," implying that our beauty does not stay the same – but is fleeting or comes to an end. We should not rely on our outer beauty to attract and keep a man. We should be working to beautify our inner beings. The verse ends with "but a woman who fears the Lord, she shall be praised." The meaning of the word fear in this context is to be in reverential awe or to have a tremendous amount of respect for. A woman who holds the Lord in high respect, this is a woman who is to be praised or admired; the kind of woman that every single lady should strive to be.

CHAPTER 14

MY PERSONAL JOURNEY

I am often asked by single ladies, "What exactly did you do to prepare yourself to become a bride and wife?" Before I share my process of preparation, my disclaimer is that we are all different and are at varying stages of our walk with Christ. The areas of growth that were needed for me may not be the same for you. My suggestion for each single woman who desires to be married is to first of all seek God for yourself and ask Him for guidance and direction for your life. The Word of God says to ask and it shall be given, to seek and ye shall find. I strongly suggest that you ask of God the areas where you need to develop and grow. Then, put on your listening ears because if you ask, I am positive, He will answer.

During my season of preparation, there were some specific things that I did to prepare myself to become a wife. I share those steps in the next chapter. And there were areas in my life where I knew I needed to either heal or grow. During the initial phase of my process, I prayed and asked God to shine a light into those dark areas of my heart and my life and prepare me to be not only a wife but a mother as well. Over time, areas of my life that needed to be dealt with were revealed to me.

There were three major areas that God showed me I needed to deal with: 1) trust, 2) self-esteem, and 3) submission. One issue at a time, I began to seek God to guide me to a place of maturity in those areas where I was weak. I prayed, fasted, read books, sought out Godly counsel, and began my path of growth one day at a time.

Learning to Trust Again

One of the first areas that God began to deal with me on was my inability to trust people – men in particular. I was the kind of person who never trusted that people's motives and desires were pure. I felt like if someone was being nice to me, "Why are they being nice? Do they want something from me?" I also had a hard time trusting that people would follow through on their word or promise to me. I'm sure I was not born this way, and am confident my trust issues were born out of things that happened to me in my childhood, adolescence, and teen years.

My first memory of my trust being violated was about the age of either five or six. I was at the age where I was allowed to cross the street by myself in the small tight-knit community where I lived. I was instructed to deliver a package to one of my older cousins who lived down the street from my grandparents. I delivered the package to my cousin who was home alone at the time. We laughed and played while I was there. Before leaving the house I remember him pulling my shorts down and touching my genitalia with his hand and penetrating me with his finger. I had no idea what he was doing. When he was done, he told me not to tell anybody. I said okay and left the house, and I remember thinking, "Don't tell anybody what? That was stupid." Because I had no idea what had just happened to me.

At some point after this incident, when I was taught about appropriate and inappropriate touch, I remember thinking, "What you are telling me not to let somebody do to me, has already happened." As a child, I recall feeling horrible that I had allowed something bad to happen to me. I also could not comprehend why someone would do such a thing. I dealt with knowing that I had been violated by tucking this information in a corner of my mind and forgetting that it had ever happened to me. I went through the rest of my childhood, adolescence, and teen years as if it never happened.

This incident was the beginning of my trust issues as they relate to men. As I grew older, I was never really comfortable around boys or men and always wondered, if given the opportunity, would they violate me? I never correlated my awkwardness with the opposite sex or my inability to trust with the fact that I had been violated at such a young age. This revelation did not come until years later when I was praying that God would heal me in areas that needed to be healed so that I may be whole for my husband.

The first issue that rose to the surface was dealing with the fact that I had been abused when I was a child. This incident started coming back to me over time in my adulthood. After suppressing this memory for years, on various occasions I remember being home during the daytime and watching different talk shows. For a time, it seemed as if every talk show that I watched profiled victims of some form of child abuse and sexual abuse in particular. These were some of the saddest, perhaps most severe cases of molestation and incest, that I had ever heard of. I remember thinking, was I really violated because many of these people were violated more than once over long periods of time by people that they knew, loved, and interacted with on a regular basis. I really did not hear about anyone who was touched inappropriately one time by a cousin that she knew but rarely interacted with. I began to doubt if my little incident even was to be categorized as abuse. This prompted me to read several books about child abuse and sexual molestation.

Through my research, I learned that I in fact was a victim of sexual molestation, even if it was only one time. This prompted me to seek God for direction as to how I should handle how I was feeling about what happened to me. Many thoughts went through my mind, such as: was I his only victim? Had he violated other children? If I report him to the authorities, will this divide my family? If I open up about this will people even believe me since it was so long ago? On any given day, I wavered between confronting my cousin, telling my mother and grandmother, or reporting him to the authorities. I was extremely confused and conflicted on my course of action. At times, I felt like I would go insane from confusion and not knowing what to do.

These feelings literally brought me to my knees and I prayed fervently asking God, "What should I do?" For weeks, I was consumed with praying about the abuse and asking for direction. I prayed, fasted – fasted and prayed. As I was praying one night, a still, small voice whispered in my spirit that I needed to forgive. The Lord spoke to me through my prayers and told me that my answer was not in forgetting what happened to me, but forgiving my cousin for what he did to me. This became my prayer that God would soften my heart toward my cousin, that God would give me strength to forgive him and move forward in my life. As I prayed that God would soften my heart toward him, God revealed to me that my cousin was approximately seven years older than me and this incident happened when I was approximately five or six years old – which meant that my cousin was only 12 or 13 years old at the time. I realized that although he was older than me, he was yet a child himself when this incident happened. I found that I actually began feeling sorry for my cousin thinking that at some point, maybe he was violated or exposed to some sort of indecent adult material to put that sort of thought in his mind at such a young age.

I began to not only pray that God would give me the strength to forgive, but I began to pray for my cousin that God would heal him. This was a pivotal moment in the area of trust for me and very freeing. Instead of wanting vengeance for the person who had violated me at such a young age, I actually prayed that God would heal him from those things that had him bound.

From this, I learned that everyone who enters my life deserves a clean slate, that I should not expect the worst of them and then be surprised if they actually showed me something different. I grew to expect the best in people and if they showed me otherwise, well that is their problem and not mine – continue to expect the good in people.

Self-esteem Merry-go-round

As a child, I remember always getting compliments regarding how pretty I was and that I was a very nice child. When I looked at myself in the mirror, I never saw pretty or ugly – I never thought about being dark-skinned or that I was not light-skinned; I didn't notice that I had big eyes or a big nose, I just saw me and was pleased with what I saw.

As I got older, began puberty and started to mature, my looks changed. I didn't receive as many compliments on my looks and I began to notice at school that most all of the boys seemed to be attracted to the light-skinned or caramel skin-toned girls; and I would overhear them name these girls as the "pretty girls" and those were the ones that they wanted as girlfriends. I remember how disappointing this was for me because I felt like if I was just a tad bit lighter, maybe someone would want me as their girlfriend. At the same time, I was conflicted because I felt like nothing was wrong with my dark skin other than the fact that the guys that I grew up around seemed to not like or appreciate the darker skinned girls.

Growing up, my friends were always a diverse group – they came from varying backgrounds, some were girls and some were boys. I was never the type of girl who did not want to hang out or play with the boys, primarily because I was much older than my friends when I was actually attracted to boys in a romantic way. So while growing up, I viewed boys as cool friends and even the ones who were considered my "boyfriends," I really was more interested in friendship than anything else. Because of this friendship I had with boys, I could always get insight into a particular boy I was interested in as a boyfriend.

I recall an incident during my early teen years where I was interested in a friend of one of my male friends. I told him that I kind of liked his friend and to find out if his friend was interested in me as a potential girlfriend. I remember a couple of weeks passing and I would ask my friend, "Did you ask him?"

He would respond something like, "No, not yet – I forgot…"

Eventually, my friend finally told me, "I did ask him, and he said" then my friend paused and asked me, "do you really want to know what he said?"

My heart sank and I responded, "Is it something bad?"

He responded "No, not really bad – but, I don't

know if you really want to hear it."

I remember hesitating and then saying, "Yes, I really do want to know what he said."

My friend told me that his friend said that I was a really nice person, and kind of cute, but he didn't like me as a girlfriend because he didn't really like dark-skinned girls. I was speechless and was thinking, "Wow, really?"

From that point, I don't really remember how I responded to my friend, but I do remember him saying something nice to me I just don't remember exactly what he said. From this point on in my teen years, I was of the mindset that I will be lucky if anyone decent wants me as their girlfriend. This was a major blow to my self-esteem. Following this incident, I guess I was pretty lucky – because not long after, someone at my school did want me as his girlfriend and I was fortunate enough to have a boyfriend for most of my high school years. For me, this was a bit of a self-esteem pick-me-up.

During my 10th grade year, I tried out and made the girls basketball team. I had never played basketball competitively before making the team. I was, however, a huge basketball fan and watched college and professional basketball religiously. To help me during basketball tryouts, I checked out a book from the library to learn basketball terms and basic drills. This book helped tremendously, because I knew what the coach and assistant coach were talking about when they said stuff like, "man-to-man defense and zone defense."

Because I had never played basketball competitively, I didn't have basketball or even athletic shoes. I purchased some no- name gym shoes from a strip mall boutique that I would pass every day walking to and from school. The shoes were no more than $10 at the time, because I asked my stepfather for $10 and this covered the cost of the shoes, including taxes. I wasn't sure that I would make the team being that I had never actually played team basketball. I do remember going to practice every day, trying hard and maintaining a positive, teachable attitude. Making my high school girls basketball team was a major self-esteem boost for me. I did not care that I did not play very much, just being a part of the team made me feel good about myself because I had a goal to make the team and in fact had done so.

Later that same school year, I tried out for the majorette squad in the marching band. I had dreamed of being a majorette in my high school band since I was a little girl. I had long ties to my high school – my mother attended the high school, both of her brothers and sisters attended as well. One of my aunts was a part of the marching band and I remember going to the football games on Friday nights to support the home team and more importantly, to watch the half time show. I loved the Mardi Gras season and was absolutely elated when I would hear people yell, "HERE COMES BLOUNT – THE NEXT BAND IS BLOUNT!" As a little girl, I remember being mesmerized by the majorettes – these pretty girls led the band. And they were all hues ranging from high yellow to dark brown. I would look at the various skin tones of the majorettes and pay particular attention to the darker skinned ones thinking,

"She is so pretty, if she can do this, I can too." This made my heart flutter in excitement.

When I started majorette tryouts, as hard as I tried, I was not very good. I recall thinking, "I want to make this line so bad, what can I do to give myself a competitive edge?" Then I remembered that a former majorette lived down the street from me – she was arguably one of the best twirlers in my school's majorette history. I remember smiling to myself and thinking, "Ask her to help you."

One day after tryouts I was particularly frustrated. I went down the street to her house. I was so nervous, I was shaking. My mind kept telling me, "She is too busy. She is not going to have time to help you." But my heart kept saying, "You will never know if you don't ask her."

So I kept walking until I reached her front door and rang the door bell. Her mother answered the door. I asked if she was home, and she was. When she came to the door, I don't know how I verbalized it, but I told her that I was trying out to be a majorette and wanted to know if she would teach me the drills. Her face lit up and she said something like, "I would be honored to help you!"

I was a little surprised and shocked. I have no idea how I responded. I just remember her telling me what days and times to come to her house for us to practice. I made the majorette line, and words cannot describe what this accomplishment did for my self-esteem and my morale as a person. I remember being so happy and thinking, "You can do anything that you put your mind to – just never be afraid to open your mouth and ask for help."

I enjoyed my final two years of high school to the fullest. My senior year, I was the head majorette/dancing girl and had a boyfriend. I had been accepted into my first choice university; and had been offered partial scholarships to two other colleges. For the first time in my life, I really looked forward to what the future had in store for me.

Once I entered college, I was in a different city, a different state, around new people and felt as if my self-esteem issues were behind me. Despite having a few lows, I had experienced some major successes during my teen and high school years and overall was in a good place. The final light-skinned versus dark-skinned challenge for mc happened early in my college years. As I waited for one of my classes to begin, a guy on campus approached me and started a conversation. He mentioned that he had seen me around campus and was glad to finally have the opportunity to meet me. I was flattered because this guy was quite handsome and tall – very in line with how I like my man and I had never even noticed him! Needless to say, he ended up with my phone number, and we became friends. As our friendship progressed, we had a discussion about skin tone and our preference in dating. I shared that I really didn't have a preference, but if I had to make a choice it would be to date someone who was brown or dark-skinned. I also shared that I was of the impression that dark-skinned guys seemed to not want to date dark-skinned girls and that light-skinned guys seemed to avoid us like the plague; and that us dark girls just had it hard all around. He then shared that he was *only* attracted to dark-skinned girls and had always dated dark girls; and was not sure about my theory concerning dark-skinned guys being that he was a light-skinned guy, but that if it was true, then they were crazy because the blacker the berry the sweeter the juice! I was speechless and actually quite flattered.

Our friendship never blossomed into a relationship because I learned that he was quite the ladies man on campus and was "friends" with several of us dark girls. We remained friends for a time. But, what I learned from his friendship and our conversation was that regardless of what my reality was about skin tone and how I or others felt about my skin tone, that beauty was in the eye of the beholder and I should not allow someone else's negative feelings toward my dark skin affect my self-esteem.

During my season of preparation, at times my past self-esteem issues would rise to the surface. I noticed that my insecurities were strongest when I was preparing for or participating in a wedding. I would think, "What is wrong with me? Why is no one attracted to me?" "If *she* can attract a husband, Lord knows I should be able to." "Here I am once again, the bridesmaid and not the bride." Single ladies, do any of these thoughts sound familiar?

I was finally liberated from my insecurities about myself and the fact that I sometimes felt that I was unattractive to men when I heard a message on TV by Bishop T.D. Jakes. The message was about sisters,

Rachel and Leah (Genesis 29:15-35; 30:1-24 NKJV). And how Jacob wanted Rachel but was tricked into marrying Leah in order to marry Rachel. Bishop Jakes ministered around the sister Leah who is viewed as the less attractive sister, but she is the sister that God looked upon and saw that she was unloved and blessed her to bear Jacob his first four sons. I remember Bishop Jakes saying that there is a blessing in being "Leah." He stated that as a woman who may feel that she is less attractive to men to thank God for the protection; that God has you wrapped in a cocoon and is protecting you until the God-ordained man comes along. I shouted and cried in my living room as I heard this message. The message was so on time for me and what I was feeling. From that point on, I have never had issues, insecurities or reservations about my looks, my self-worth, or whether or not I am attractive. After years of struggling and dealing with self-esteem issues, this part of my past was finally behind me.

Submission Learned

During my season of preparation, the final area that God revealed to me was submission. I never thought that I had an issue with authority or submitting to leadership. I read the book *Liberated through Submission* by P.B. Wilson and really felt that I would not have a problem submitting to my husband as long as he was submitted to Christ. I was of the mindset, "I got this. I have no issues with submission."

My issue with submission became apparent to me while taking a Bible class at my church. At the end of the session for the class, the teacher allowed all of us students to share. There was an elderly lady in the class and of all the people who spoke, myself included, I remember a portion of what she said. She began by stating her desire to impart wisdom into the younger generation in the room. Then told us to appreciate our jobs and to not steal work time; that it was important to do the job that we were hired to do. To make sure that we arrive on time, eat lunch within our allotted time, and leave work at the assigned time. I valued what she had to say but didn't think much it at the time. In the days and weeks that followed, her words continued to replay and repeat in my head while I was at work – to arrive on time, eat lunch within my allotted time, and to leave at the appropriate time. After several weeks of this, her statement was like a broken record that replayed one line over and over in my mind. I can still hear her say, "Do the job that you were hired to do." This quiet but strong voice made me reevaluate my actions and attitude at work and toward leadership.

My issue with subpar leadership didn't happen overnight. The issue that I had with following poor leaders started many years earlier.

I obtained my first job when I was 15 years old. I started out volunteering for a community center because I wanted to be in a pageant, and I needed volunteer hours. I volunteered at the community center that was around the corner from my house. After two, maybe three days of me volunteering, the center director was so impressed at my commitment to volunteering that he recommended that I go to the local Job Training Partnership Act (JTPA 1982) employment office to apply for a summer job and he would simultaneously put in a request to have a youth worker assigned to his facility – with the understanding that I would be his summer student worker.

After filling out the application for the summer job, the interviewer noticed that I could type. She stated that they had an emergency at a job site that needed someone who could type and asked if I would be interested. I explained that I already had a job at the community center. The lady stated that she would speak to the center director and make sure that it was okay to reassign me somewhere else since I knew how to type and that she would send him over two boys to work at the recreation center. This began my journey into the world of work.

Early on I noticed that many adults in the workplace were dishonest. As a youth, my first day always consisted of learning the rules and basics concerning the job. I was told what time to come in, what time to leave, and what time to have lunch. As a teenager, I did what I was told – in the beginning. It didn't take long for me to catch on to the workplace improprieties that were taking place – like coming in a little late, leaving a little early, and having a long lunch on occasion. As the years passed and with each job, I got better at "playing" on work time. My motto was, "While the cat's away, the mouse will play." I did not have this attitude toward workplace rules when I initially started working. On my first job, years earlier, I did exactly as I was told. My negative attitude toward workplace rules and authority came about as I watched year after year and workplace after workplace, certain people get away with stretching the rules and they seemed to be rewarded and promoted for their work and there were others who followed the rules but never seemed to progress very much in the work place. Witnessing bad behavior being unknowingly rewarded not only bothered, but angered me. As a result, I adopted many of the same ways such as: slight tardiness, long lunches, and handling personal business on work time.

I operated in this manner for years as a working professional; and was rarely, if ever, chastised for my bad behavior since it was quite the norm. I was always a high performer as it related to my job, which could also explain why my bad behavior was often overlooked. In retrospect I realize that I assimilated into my environment and was thriving on various jobs, but I was operating far beneath the level that God had intended as a representative for Him in the workplace. I'm certain this is why the words of the elderly lady in my Bible class resonated with me so much. I was being a poor witness of Christ in the workplace with my behavior.

As I began to reevaluate my behavior at work, God was working with me on an even deeper level. Reading *Liberated through Submission* was part of my preparation to become a wife. This was one of several books that I read to get me ready for marriage. I had heard that there were married ladies who had issue with submitting to their husbands; and the problems that their rebellious attitudes caused in the marriages. I myself knew of several single ladies who took issue with the taboo topic of submission. I figured I would be proactive and deal with any issues I had concerning submission. I therefore took heed to the advice of author P.B. Wilson, who also wrote the book *Knight in Shining Armor...*" – which is the book that I previously mentioned started me on my path of preparing for my God-ordained husband.

I finished the book actually knowing and understanding what submission is and what it is not. When I started reading the book, I thought submission was a husband's right to have uncontested rule and reign over his wife. I thought that by being a submissive wife that a woman must be a weak person. I thought that submission in marriage was a husband making all of the decisions and the wife having no voice or say-so whatsoever in the business matters of the family. I also felt that I had no issue with submission because my marriage would be 50/50; and that neither one of us would have rule or reign over the other one. The decision-making would involve the both of us. I was strictly thinking about submission as it pertained to a married couple – a wife being submissive to her husband. My mindset was that I get the concept and would have no problem submitting to my husband as long as he was submitted to Christ.

The Lord revealed to me as I was working through my workplace issues that the root cause of my problem was my ignorance concerning submission and my lack of respect for authority. The Lord showed me that the issue that I had in the workplace would transfer right into my marriage unless I dealt with the root of the problem and that was learning how to be submissive to authority. I prayed for clarity, strength, and the ability to be a submissive spirit because the Lord knew my heart and the fact that I really had a problem with incompetent leadership.

As with the other areas that God dealt with me on during my season of preparation, my issues with submission were gradually resolved. Over time, I transformed into a model employee whether my superior was around or not. Every day that I entered my job site, I carried the mindset with me that I was working for and representing God. I no longer concerned myself with what my co-workers were doing wrong or even my boss, for that matter, and was focused on me and being the best representation of Christ that I could be. The scripture in Colossians 3:23 (NKJV), "And whatsoever ye do, do it heartily, as to the Lord, and not unto men;" became my workplace mantra. I memorized and meditated on this word. At one job that was particularly trying, I taped the scripture to my computer monitor to constantly remind me of my purpose for being there.

The following areas: inability to trust, poor self-esteem, and submission/issues with authority were strongholds in my life. These were the areas God showed me that I needed to work on and work through before I was a complete person, ready for marriage.

As you seek God for growth and deliverance, He will reveal to you what areas in your life need to be dealt with prior to your marriage. If you are dealing with strongholds; generational curses; physical, mental, or sexual abuse that happened in your past; and/or negative seeds that were planted in your mind as a child or teenager, don't be surprised if these are the areas that are brought to the forefront to be dealt with. God wants you whole, as in W-H-O-L-E, not H-O-L-E in marriage. And the way to becoming a whole person is to deal with those painful areas that you have tucked away in the back of your mind and forgotten about. I once heard the statement, "Be careful what you say to a child – when they become adults, this is their inner voice." I have never heard a truer statement. I add to that statement, "What happens in our childhood and adolescence will either make or break us as adults."

CHAPTER 15

ON THE ROAD TO SUCCESS

In addition to me praying and seeking God to deal with those dark areas of my life, there were other things that I did to prepare myself to become a wife.

I.

Early in the process, I began to *separate* myself from the "group," (single women). I felt that a single woman could not help me on my path to being married. I did not hang out with a lot of single women, especially those who were moaning and complaining that there were no good men. Because I was seeking to be around women who were where I wanted to be – married, I made a conscience choice not to be actively involved in the Singles Ministry at my church. I did attend some of the Singles Ministry social events and Bible studies, but was never led to fervently serve with the group.

II.

I began to *seek out and surround myself with married women* whom I could learn from. Women who had solid, Christian marriages that possessed qualities I could model my own after. I was like a sponge. I soaked up everything these married women had to offer in terms of advice, tips, and tricks of the trade of being married. I never asked any of these women to be a mentor to me. I watched, listened, and observed their behavior as married women. Whenever I had a one-on-one moment with a married lady, I wanted to talk about marriage. I would ask them questions: How did they meet their husband? How long did they date before they were married? I also inquired about married life in general.

III.

I *stopped dating*. (PERIOD.) After a time, I opened myself up to being courted, but I did not casually date. I once heard the statement, as it relates to dating that when you date, you are practicing for a divorce. When I initially heard this, I was puzzled. However, after much thought and contemplation, I came to the realization and agreement that dating was practicing for a divorce. When you casually date, you are more likely to jump from one relationship and sex partner to the next if something does not go exactly as you like—the perfect model for a divorce. In addition, my stance on dating was that casual dating is a distraction. It distracts you from those things that are important, like working on you and becoming closer to God by developing a consistent prayer life.

IV.

I grew in my *prayer life.* I've always been a praying person – during my season of preparation, I became a prayer warrior. During my prayer and personal devotion time is where I would receive direction and clarity concerning those things that worried or troubled me. I would labor in prayer for my marriage and any other areas that came to mind.

V.

I *read books* about marriage and preparing to be a wife. I read books about healing and forgiveness and began to study the Bible in the area of marriage and love. I studied what God said about love and what God said about marriage. Some of the book titles that I read that had the most profound effect on me were: *Knight in Shining Armor, Liberated through Submission,* and *Betrayal's Baby* by P.B. Wilson, *The Three Battlegrounds* by Francis Frangipane and *Making Your Husband Feel Loved,* compiled by Betty Malz. There were many other books that I read, but the aforementioned had the greatest impact. A couple of other books that I read either right before or shortly after I married that were impactful were, *The Power of a Praying Wife* by Stormie Omartian and *After Every Wedding Comes a Marriage"* by Florence Littauer.

VI.

I began to get my *finances* in order. I purchased my first house and started diligently paying off my car note and paying down my credit cards and student loan debt. I felt like, if I am requiring that my husband have good credit, a stable income, and wisdom in his finances then I should have all those attributes as well. I came to believe that I could not have an expectation for my husband that I could not fulfill myself.

I previously discussed that during my season of preparation, I suffered a financial setback. I launched a business that incurred a considerable amount of debt and was not making enough income to cover all of my business expenses. As a result I incurred judgments for the debts. Prior to getting married, I refinanced my house and paid off my judgments. I did not want to bring a bad debt into the marriage.

VII.

And lastly, as a result of reading *The Power of a Praying Wife*, I started specifically *praying* for my husband. As the book suggests, I prayed for my husband in 30 areas of his life; and also prayed for him in many other areas as the spirit gave me unction. I used the principle of Romans 4:17 (NIV). I called those things which did not exist as though they did. I prayed that my husband – I did not use the word "future" — would be a mighty man of God, a man of valor, a man who loved and respected his mother and held his family as a priority, a man who would love me as Christ loved the church, a man I could trust with my heart, a man who had his finances in order, a man who would respect my decision to not have sex until we married— one who would respect the anointing and call of God on my life.

My Vow of Celibacy

When I began my journey of preparation, I made a decision to not have sex until I married. When I made this decision, I was not a virgin. I simply felt that sex outside of marriage, like dating, was a distraction. Shortly after making my vow of no sex until marriage, I recall having an issue with lust; it seemed as if I lusted after almost every man I saw. My lustful thoughts became so intense and bizarre that I shared with one of my cousins who was my roommate at the time some of the thoughts I was having. I also shared that several of the men that I had thoughts about, I wasn't even physically attracted to; and this puzzled me initially. We both laughed at how bizarre my thoughts were and she shrugged them off. I knew that something was going on.

Because of the frequency and severity of the thoughts, I knew that the enemy was trying to invade my mind with impure images and thoughts to spur me to break my vow of celibacy. During this period, I recall that I continually prayed about the lustful thoughts I was having and because I wasn't attracted to some of the men, I knew that the lustful thoughts invading my mind were an attack of the enemy. I overcame these lustful thoughts by praying the Word. Every time a lustful thought came to mind, I would say "Let this mind be in you which was also in Christ Jesus." I would ask God to renew my mind and my thoughts. At that time in my life, I was not as learned in the Word and did not know that this scripture in Philippians 2:5 (NKJV) was referring to the humble mind of Christ but now feel as though God answered my prayer because I was praying from a sincere and earnest heart.

The lustful thoughts did not immediately go away – I do remember that they became less frequent and I no longer had episodes of feeling like I was being overtaken by my thoughts. After that, every now and then, a lustful thought would cross my mind and I would declare that I had the mind of Christ and that I was meditating on those things which were lovely and pure to the point where I no longer had lustful thoughts while on my journey of preparation.

My Heart's Desire

I had a specific prayer request about my future husband respecting my decision to not have sex until I was married – this was extremely important to me. When I made my vow of celibacy, I had repented of my sin of having sex outside of marriage and vowed that I would remain pure until I married. During one of my prayer times, I was lamenting to God that my decision to not have sex before I was married would not be acceptable to any grown man in this day and age. I continued to tell God that from past experience there is absolutely NO man out there—Christian or not—who would date or be engaged to a woman and not have sex. That still, calm voice, the Holy Spirit, revealed to me that I will know my husband because he will not only respect my decision to remain celibate until I married, but would have the exact same vow!

The relief that I felt is hard to put into words.

My inward being was literally shouting. More than anything, I did not want to break God's heart; and at that point, I no longer stressed over whether or not I would be able to live up to my vow of celibacy. Because I knew that my God-ordained husband would be aligned with me and my desire to remain celibate until marriage.

PART III: WAIT FOR BOAZ

CHAPTER 16

BEWARE OF THE COUNTERFEIT

Counterfeit (defined) – made in imitation so as to be passed off fraudulently or deceptively as genuine; a close likeness; imposter, pretender; to resemble.

Approximately 2 ½ years into my process, I became engaged to my college sweetheart. At that time, we had been dating off and on for about six years. I was absolutely ecstatic. It is hard to describe in words how I felt. My fiancé had accompanied me to work that day. I was the event manager for a big sporting event that happened earlier in the day. Afterward, we decided to grab a bite to eat at a restaurant near my house.

We were eating, talking, and having a good time. I was thinking, "Okay this is the day after Christmas. He didn't propose on Christmas, maybe he is not going to do it."

At that point, I was okay with him not doing the

whole marriage proposal thing on Christmas day as I had envisioned he would. Then to my surprise, our waiter brought out a dessert tray, placed it in front of me and said, "Congratulations. Enjoy your dessert."

Puzzled, I looked at my boyfriend as I took the cover off the dessert. There, on the tray, was a ring box. I opened the box and one of the most gorgeous diamond rings I had ever seen smiled back at me. He then proposed, and I of course said, "Yes."

I was about to be three years into my commitment of preparing myself to become a wife. *Wow, what perfect timing!* I thought.

However, I would soon realize that this relationship and engagement were simply not of God. Saying that the engagement was not of God is nothing negative against the man to whom I was engaged. He was a wonderful person; however, the two of us being married was not God's design.

My fiancé was a Christian, college-educated, handsome, hardworking, articulate, honest. He was just an overall good guy. He possessed all of the top qualities on my list. In the natural, my thoughts were, "It doesn't get much better than this. I'm engaged to be married to a guy I know, love, and trust. We have history, being that we dated in college." I was well on my way to becoming a wife.

Despite everything looking perfect in the natural, deep down something never quite felt right about our engagement. Initially, I didn't understand what I was feeling. I was thinking, "Maybe I'm feeling this way since we are in this long-distance relationship." However, as time passed, the fact that we were not ordained to be together became more apparent. I never quite understood why we argued about nothing all the time. We simply could not agree on anything.

I prayed that God would somehow work this relationship out and allow us to be together. The harder I prayed, the more problems we began to have. In prayer one night, I finally asked God, "What is it? Why are we having so many problems in this relationship? Why can we not agree on basic things? Why do I still have an unsettled feeling in my spirit about this engagement?"

That still, small voice of God responded, "Terry, you are having problems because this relationship is not meant to be. You are looking at how perfect the relationship is in the natural, and I want to bless you with much more."

This revelation hit me like a ton of bricks because I knew what I had to do—and that was to break off the engagement. Initially, I did not accept this revelation. I was thinking, "God this can work – right?" Not only was God showing me in the spirit that my fiancé was not the ordained husband for me, but the long distance between the two of us proved to be too great to bear. Some say, "Distance makes the heart grow fonder." I believe in our situation that the distance simply caused us to grow farther apart. In the two years that we were together, we physically saw each other two times.

During those brief encounters that we were together we had sexual relations. I struggled with this because I had taken a vow of celibacy when I began my process. And the Lord had really spoken to me that my God-ordained husband would respect my decision to not have sex until after marriage. My ex-fiancé was not in agreement with my vow at all. He felt that since we were in a committed relationship and were on our way to being married, that there was nothing wrong with sex before marriage. This weighed heavily on my conscience because I knew that I had made a vow before God and that I was in a relationship with a man who clearly did not respect my vow. For me, this was a red flag. A man who knew my heart and my desire to please God and did not respect this but in fact, attempted to justify the sin – was not okay with me.

I so struggled with what I knew that I ultimately had to do, that my disobedience drove me to sickness. About a year after my engagement, I became so stressed out over the fact that I knew I had to end it, that I began having debilitating migraine headaches. My migraine headaches were so bad, that I sought medical attention and was put on medicine to control the headaches. At that time, I was paying $10 per pill for migraine medication, and the pharmacist would only dispense four pills at a time. I was instructed to only take the pill if necessary and right as I felt a migraine headache coming on. I remember praying to God that not only could I could not afford to be sick, but the migraine pills made me so sick I began to debate which was worse, the actual migraine or the side effects from taking the migraine medication.

It took me about a year from the time God revealed this to me, to officially break off the engagement and relationship. Besides burying my mother, this was one of the hardest things that I ever had to do in my life. I remember the phone conversation sometime in the fall of 2002. I was nearing the end of the paralegal program that I was in and felt like this was a good time to dig my heels in and do what I needed to do and officially end the relationship. I'm not sure what led me there, but I remember telling my fiancé that as the year was coming to an end, I was beginning to turn a new leaf and that after praying and seeking God for direction that I was dropping the dead weight from my life. I further clarified that he was a part of what I felt was dead weight in my life. He, of course, thought I was joking and just upset again, but I reiterated that I was serious and that our relationship was done. After that conversation, I did not call or email him again. He soon realized that I was serious because his calls became few and far in between.

The engagement to my ex-fiancé reminded me of a warning from P.B. Wilson in her book *Knight in Shining Armor* and that is to beware of the counterfeit as you are preparing yourself for your husband. During your process of preparation, men will be attracted to the "new" you. You must guard your heart and remain prayerful at all times that you are using your spiritual eyesight when it comes to accepting a mate. Things may look great in the natural, as they did for me, but this particular person may not be who God has for you.

I never wanted to admit that my fiancé was

indeed a counterfeit, because I cared so deeply for him. However, on the day when I finally made up in my mind that I would officially end our engagement and association, I packaged the engagement ring and a pair of diamond earrings that he had purchased for me and got them ready to be mailed back to him. This act was extremely freeing for me. I felt as if a weight had been released from my life, like a heavy piece of baggage that I was carrying around had finally been dropped. I informed my ex-fiancé that I would be returning the diamond ring and earrings to him and he insisted that I keep them, so I did. However, about a year later I mailed that package to him.

After I officially broke off my engagement, I began what I call my process of restoration. I repented for my disobedience and being slow to act when God made it plain what I needed to do; I left my sin at the altar, and prayed for restoration. I gave my heart back to God and recommitted to my process of preparation. At this time I was five years into my "preparation process." As I journeyed through my year of restoration, an interesting thing happened. I was hanging out at the church after a dance ministry practice, talking and socializing with the other ladies who worked in the dance ministry with me. We were talking about everything and nothing. In the vicinity of where we were talking was an older employee of the church who often assisted the ministry with facility requests. He made a simple yet profound statement to me, which was, "Terry, if you give that ring back I guarantee you that God will bless you with somebody else." His statement baffled me a little, because I had not told very many people that I had ended my engagement and as a result had practically told no one that my ex-fiancé wanted me to keep the ring even though we were no longer together.

For a couple of days, I thought long and hard about what the elder said and realized that whether he knew it or not, his words were divine – I realized that my keeping the ring was an ungodly tie to my ex-fiancé. His words are what prompted me to actually mail the ring and diamond earrings back to my ex-fiancé. Not long after I returned the engagement ring and earrings (less than a year), I met the man who would later become my husband.

My encounter with the counterfeit reminds me of the story of half brothers, Ishmael and Isaac. My analogy is that Ishmael was the "distraction" [counterfeit] and Isaac was the "promise" [real thing]. (Genesis 15:2-6; 16:1-4; 18:9-14; 21:1-7 NKJV)

Genesis 15:2-6

Abram was lamenting to God, that he did not have any children and that his inheritance would be passed on to a servant in his household. God made a covenant with Abram that his seed shall be as plenteous as the stars in the sky. Abram believed and trusted God's word regarding his offspring. This took a tremendous amount of faith on Abram's part being that he had NO children at the time of this covenant. The Amplified version of the Bible says that Abram believed in (trusted in, relied on, remained steadfast to) the Lord, and He counted it to him as righteousness (right standing with God).

We must also be this way when we know that God has promised us something. We must trust in, rely on, and remain steadfast to that what the Lord has promised us.

Genesis 16:1-4

Sarai, Abram's wife, grew impatient waiting for God to fulfill His promise to Abram and convinced Abram to take her servant, Hagar to bear him children because the children would belong to Sarai. Abram agreed and took on Hagar as a wife; subsequently impregnating her. During Hagar's pregnancy, contention grew between Sarai and Hagar. Hagar eventually ran away from Sarai, but later returned to her master. Hagar gave birth to a son, Ishmael, when Abram was eighty-six years old.

None of this was God's plan or desire for Sarai and Abram; this was Sarai's plan – a result of her impatience. When God has promised us something, we must be patient and wait for God's timing. This is imperative not only in the area of a spouse, but in any area where we are waiting for the promise of God to manifest.

Genesis 18:9-14

Sometime later, the Lord reminds Abraham (formerly Abram) of his promise stating that at the

114

appointed time his wife shall bear him a son. Sarah (formerly Sarai) overheard this and doubted, laughing to herself at God's promise to Abram. The Lord asks, "Why is Sarah laughing?" ....the Lord then says, "Is there anything too hard for God?"

In other words, God is saying, "If I promised it, I will fulfill it." My word to the single ladies is to not get impatient waiting on God to bless you with a mate. Don't settle for the counterfeit, that is not God's plan or desire for your life. Sarah and Abraham's impatience brought forth Ishmael; a child who was indeed blessed by God, but, was not Abraham's promise from God. All too often single ladies find themselves in a precarious situation, like Sarah and Hagar, because of good intentions that are not the will of God.

Genesis 21:1-7

The Lord visits Sarah, just as He promised and she becomes pregnant. Sarah gives birth to Isaac in her old age. Then laughs and is so overwhelmed with joy that she says, "God has made me to laugh; all who hear will laugh with me ...who would have said to Abraham that Sarah would nurse children at the breast? For I have borne him a son in his old age." Abraham was one hundred years old when Sarah gave birth to Isaac. Isaac's name means "laugh."

Just as God had promised, he blessed Abraham with a son. And both Sarah and Abraham were overjoyed with happiness and laughter. Regardless of how long it takes, God's timing is perfect timing. We must not limit God to "time." God operates in "seasons." The Word of God says, "To everything there is a season, a time for every purpose under heaven" (Ecclesiastes 3:1 NKJV). At the appointed season, Sarah became pregnant and gave birth to Isaac. Let Sarah be an encouragement to every single lady who is waiting and believing God for a husband, that no matter how long it takes, you will wait for God. God wants to bless you in such a way that your heart will be overcome with joy, and others around you will laugh and rejoice with you.

Don't accept that counterfeit. And don't try to make a relationship happen that is not God's will for your life; wait for God to move. God does not need your help. And lastly, remember that the counterfeit is made to look and feel like the real thing, but it isn't.

CHAPTER 17

RUTH, A GODLY EXAMPLE

One of my favorite scriptures in the Bible to read when I was single was the book of Ruth. I often found comfort and encouragement in the story of Ruth, the Moabite woman, whose husband died and she travelled to a foreign land with her mother-in-law in hopes of a better life as a widow in a different country.

I highly encourage single women to read the book of Ruth anytime you find that you need encouragement during your season of singleness.

Background

At the beginning of the book of Ruth, we learn that there is a famine in the land. A man by the name of Elimelech, his wife Naomi, and their two sons move to the country of Moab. Elimelech dies. Both of their sons marry Moabite women, and the sons eventually die, leaving behind their wives, Orpah and Ruth, with the mother Naomi. Naomi got word that the famine was over and decided to return to her native land. She urged the wives to go back to their fathers. Orpah did. Ruth stayed with Naomi (Ruth 1 NKJV).

Ruth 2

During those times, the corners of fields were not to be reaped, and the sheaf accidentally left behind was not to be carried away, according to the law of Moses (Leviticus 19:9; 23:22; Deuteronomy 24:21 NKJV). They were to be left for the poor to glean. Similar laws were given regarding vineyards and olive yards. Ruth obtained Naomi's permission to go out and glean.

Ruth humbled herself and gleaned in the field to make a living for both herself and Naomi. She was not idle, waiting for something to come to her. Instead, she got up and made something happen for herself. While gleaning in the field, Boaz noticed Ruth and inquired about her, asking, "Whose young woman is this?" When he learned that Ruth was with Naomi, he instructed her to not go to another field to glean and to stay close to his servants. He instructed the men to leave her alone. He also instructed the men to purposefully allow grains to fall from the bundles for Ruth to glean. She was also allowed to eat with his workers. Ruth found favor with Boaz – he had heard about her faithfulness to her mother-in-law, Naomi, and granted her favorable treatment as a result.

Positioned to Be Blessed

Ruth was gleaning in Boaz's field. She was in position to be blessed and was noticed by the man who owned the field, the man who would eventually be her husband. She did not go out and try to manipulate a situation; she was simply in position to be blessed working outside in a field. In the story of Ruth, there is a lesson for all single ladies, which is while you are single do not sit around with a down trodden attitude, put your hands to the plow and serve. In our American society, we always want to be served. However, when you are in a position where you choose to serve others, you are on your way to becoming a Lady-in-Waiting and thus a wife.

When I was single, I saw myself in the book Ruth; our stories different – yet, similar. As I shared earlier, my mom passed away when I was 28 years old. I took in my youngest brother who was 12 at the time, moved him from Alabama to Arizona and we both began a new life; me as a single parent/care taker of my brother and my brother as a new kid in town, a new school, a new church, and a new family dynamic. I was the sole provider and care taker for my brother and me. In essence, I was serving my mother by taking in my brother. My mother's last wish was that I move my brother to Arizona when she passed away. There were other options: I could have left my brother in Alabama with our grandmother, with our stepfather, or with one of our other brothers or sister who were all adults. I chose to be obedient to my mom even in her death by granting her last wish – I took my brother in and raised him as my own.

During the five years prior to getting married when it was my brother and I – I truly saw the hand of God in my situation. I was of the mindset that my attracting a potential husband might be a challenge because I was raising my teenage brother. I had settled in my mind that I would get married once I had raised my brother. I was in for a pleasant surprise.

Wait for Boaz

I encourage every woman who desires a husband and is wondering when marriage will happen for you, to begin preparing yourself to be a wife; to humbly take on the attitude of a servant. And just know that God wants to bless you. However, you need to be in a position to be blessed by God. There is no need to have the "I'm always the bridesmaid, never the bride" type of attitude. Don't get weary in your season of singleness. I reiterate: Use this time to work on you and serve others.

CHAPTER 18

I WAITED FOR BOAZ

I feel blessed and privileged to be married to a wonderful God-fearing man of integrity; especially since there are ladies who were single when I began my journey, who are still single. My process of preparation is unique in that there were specific things that I did to get ready to be a wife. And as I reflect on my seven-year process to becoming a wife, in addition to the things that I did to prepare myself, more importantly there was a God part in my process; and had it not been for the grace, deliverance, and favor of God, I perhaps might still be single.

My Heart Opens Up To God's Plan

A few months prior to meeting my husband, I had a huge crush on a guy at my church. I noticed this guy at a Wednesday evening Bible study then started noticing him at church on Sundays. This particular guy caught my eye because he was tall, athletic, and handsome – the way I like my men; and I was impressed that he was at a mid-week church service. Years of attending church, I have observed that not very many men attend a mid-week church service or Bible study and those who do attend are either lay-men working in the ministry or married men. When I initially saw this guy, I knew that he was either new to the ministry or visiting the church from another ministry, because I faithfully attended Bible study and had never seen him. Like most single women who notice a man they like, I got a glance at the ring finger. No ring. I was happy. I was thinking, "Thank you Jesus, thank you Lord! My ship has come in."

After observing this guy for a couple of weeks, I began to ask a couple of close friends at the church if they knew him. As a result of asking around, I learned that he was in fact new to the church and was recently divorced. My heart dropped. I thought, *Oh no Lord! I do not want to marry a man who is divorced.*

Learning that he was recently divorced did not change the way I felt. I still had a huge crush on him and prayed about it. I began to reassess the item on my "list" that said I did not want to marry someone who had been married and divorced already. After talking to God about this, I resigned that if he was in fact the one, that I could accept his divorce.

I continued admiring him from afar and a few more weeks passed. I patiently waited for him to notice me and ask me out. While waiting, I continued to discreetly ask questions and find out more about him from a few people at the church whom I trusted. I soon learned that in addition to being newly divorced, that my dream man also had a small daughter. I remember thinking, *No, no, no Lord – NO children! I do not want to marry a man who has children*. I was so disappointed that my future husband had not only been married previously, but also had a small child. I prayed and talked to God about this. I prayed and asked God to soften my heart to accept his child, if in fact, he was the one for me.

A few more weeks passed and I remember praying, "Okay God, if he is the one, I can accept that he has a child. I just don't want to have to deal with all the baby mama drama."

I continued to wait to be asked out by my future husband and just knew that it would happen any day since I had altered my list and could now accept that my future husband had been previously married and had a child. Not soon after I had altered my list and mentally scratched off my no divorce and no children requirement, I learned that my future husband would be moving out of state. I was devastated. I lamented, "God, if he is moving, who am I going to marry now? Lord why would you take me on this emotional journey just to have this man move out of state?" I was crushed, to say the least.

The Final Prophecy

A few weeks before I became acquainted with my future husband, I was at a youth ministry staff and volunteer meeting where a local youth pastor ministered to us workers then imparted a prophetic word to each of us. The words he spoke to me were on point, but none more than the statement that he made to me saying that I was NOT Leah, I was not a disadvantaged woman – God wanted me to know that I was Rachel. After hearing this, I nearly fainted. I had shared with no one my experience with being delivered from my off and on struggle with self-esteem through the message from Bishop T.D. Jakes on sisters Rachel and Leah. As the pastor spoke, I felt as if God himself was speaking directly to me and using this man as his physical representation at that moment. I was floored, speechless, and overjoyed because I felt as if God had released me into a new realm of existence. A few years earlier, I overcame my self-esteem issues from the vantage point that there was an advantage to being a disadvantaged woman – God spoke to my heart at that moment and said, "There is nothing about you that is disadvantaged."

My Time – My Season

A couple of months after my dream man and who I thought would be my husband had moved out of state, I became acquainted with Lloyd, the man I would eventually marry. I knew of Lloyd because his daughter was a part of the dance ministry – outside of communicating with him via mass email and phone calls about dance practices, dress rehearsals or dance attire, I had never talked to him or even noticed him before his daughter became a part of the children's praise dance group.

Approximately a year and a half prior to meeting Lloyd, I had met with the youth pastor at the church and informed him that my time with the ministry was coming to an end and that he should start thinking about a successor. This conversation with the youth pastor actually came about as a result of my frustration at the time with some things that were going on in the ministry, and I wanted to quit because I was fed up with the backbiting and discord. I was praying about the things that I was going through in the dance ministry and in my personal life as I was preparing for a husband; and out of my frustration told God that I just need to quit volunteering with the ministry and that if I quit, then I would have more time to devote to me. God responded in my prayer time that it was not my time to quit – that I had another year and a half with the ministry and then I would be moving on to a new season.

At the end of the dance year – and the end of my season with the ministry — we hosted a dance recital for the children and youth. The dance recital was two-fold for me: It was a culmination of the dance year, an opportunity for the children to minister in dance one last time before summer break and it was an opportunity for me to ceremoniously depart the ministry. As part of the festivities, we gave each of the dancers a certificate of achievement. At the end of the recital, among the lost and found items that were collected was one dancer's certificate.

A day or two after the recital, the dancer's father sent me an email and wanted to know if his daughter had left behind her dance certificate. I informed him that she had. In the same email, he asked me if I would be interested in going out on a date with him. I answered, "Yes, I would be." And this began my courtship with the man who would become my husband.

I have often reflected on my process of preparation and the final 12-18 months in particular and am always in awe of how God orchestrated my life so that I would be in position to be noticed by the man who would be my husband. Of the 50 certificates that we issued, only one was left behind. Lloyd had "noticed" me some months earlier, but was too shy to ask me out. He was also under the assumption that I was still engaged, but wasn't certain. At the time, Lloyd and I had a mutual friend. He began asking her questions about me; questions like, my age – he wanted to make sure that I was in the age range that he was interested in because he thought I had a very youthful appearance; was I engaged or dating; and he asked about the teenager that was always with me at church. My friend informed him that my mom had passed and I was raising my teenage brother. Lloyd told me that he was extremely impressed at the fact that despite being relatively young myself that I had taken in my younger brother. He also shared that it was apparent to him that I was taking good care of my brother, who always appeared to be a well-dressed, well-mannered young man. Lloyd did not have reservations about me as a potential wife because I had my teenage brother as a responsibility, but in fact was even more attracted to me because of the sacrifice that I was making to raise my brother.

When his daughter left behind her dance certificate, this gave him a reason to reach out to me and in the process opened the door for him to ask me out. God's timing is perfect. Lloyd mustered up the courage to ask me out not knowing that the dance recital was my last official event with the ministry and I would not return after the summer break. God knew.

The fact that I met my husband serving in the dance ministry with children and youth was divine confirmation for me. At some point in my process, in my prayer time I was expressing my concern to God and wanting to know how would I ever get noticed by a man if I was volunteering in the children and youth ministry. I asked God if I was even serving in the right capacity. I remember telling God that no one notices or even appreciates those of us who labor with the children and youth – and how will I ever catch the eye of a man if I am hidden in the youth ministry? That still voice whispered, "Terry, you are right where I need you to be." And like a child frustrated with their parent, because they do not understand what is going on, but they trust that their parent has their best interest in mind, I reluctantly replied, "Okay, I will stay the course."

The guy at my church that I had a huge crush on before I met Lloyd is not a mere coincidence; God knew that I was not ready to receive my husband. I now realize that he used the guy at my church to prepare my heart for my husband. Prior to being attracted to that guy, I did not want to marry a man who had been previously married nor did I want to marry a man who had children. This guy had recently gone through a divorce and he had a daughter. As I began to get to know Lloyd and learned that he not only had a daughter but had been previously married, I remember thinking, *Now I get it, Lord.* The sole purpose the guy at my church played in my life was to get my heart ready to receive Lloyd – he was never meant to be my husband like I thought. If I had not negotiated those items on my list – not wanting to marry someone who had been previously married and/or someone who had any children – I would not have considered Lloyd as a potential husband.

Over time, just as I became more of a Church Sister and less of a Professional Student, my list matured and I began to re-evaluate those items on my list that were desires but not must-haves. At the core of why I didn't want to marry a person with an ex-wife and/or any children was that I did not want to deal with any ex-wife or "baby mama" drama. As I got to know Lloyd, I learned that he and his ex-wife had a very amicable relationship and were both very active in parenting their daughter. If you are a single lady who is stuck on the wants and desires on your list, and are adamant that you will not settle, I strongly suggest that you critically evaluate those vain wants and desires and at least give a potential mate a chance if he meets the must-haves on your list. Would you really not consider a man as a husband who has the character that you desire because he does not possess something that you merely want but do not necessarily need to be happy?

A Shouting Moment

Lloyd and I had our first date in May; afterward we had a couple of phone conversations and agreed to go out again. Early in the courtship, I told him about my preparation process and that I did not date, that I was preparing myself to be a wife. He explained that he was preparing himself for a wife – despite the fact that he had been married before he realized that there was work that God needed to do in his life to prepare him to marry again. We both agreed that we were at a point in our lives where we did not want to waste time dating if we felt that the relationship was not going to lead to marriage. We continued getting to know each other and began to officially date in July of the same year.

The final confirmation that the man I was dating would become my husband was our conversation about sex. I explained that part of my process of preparing for my husband was that in addition to not casually dating, that I although I was not a virgin that I had made a vow to not have sex again until I was married. I remember Lloyd expressing that he was in total agreement that sex is for the marriage bed; and totally supported and respected my desire to not have sex, until we got married. Talk about a shouting moment – I was jumping up and down on the inside screaming, thank you, Lord! Thank you, Jesus!

During our dating period, we continued getting to know each other. We began to introduce the other to our family; and we set boundaries in terms of how we would date. One of the major boundaries that we established was to limit the amount of time that we spent at each other's house watching television. We both agreed that visiting to watch a movie or spend time together is very innocent when you are initially dating, but as the relationship progresses, spending this sort of quality time together opens the door for the enemy to entice us – a Christian couple – to fornicate or behave in a manner that did not edify Christ. We both agreed that we wanted to glorify God in our relationship; and would not put ourselves or the other person in a predicament that would compromise this.

My Confessions of Faith

While dating Lloyd, I emailed and shared with him my confessions of faith; which were: 1) Terry is a virtuous wife whose worth is far above rubies. The heart of her husband safely trusts her; so he will have no lack of gain. Terry does him good and not evil all the days of her life. Strength and honor are her clothing; she shall rejoice at all times. Terry opens her mouth with wisdom, and on her tongue is the law of kindness. Terry watches over the ways of her household, and does not eat the bread of idleness. Her children rise up and call her blessed; her husband also, and he praises her. Proverbs 31:10-12, 25-28 (NKJV) 2) Terry is an excellent wife who is the crown of her husband. Proverbs 12:4a (NKJV) 3) Terry's husband renders to her the affection due her, and likewise Terry to her husband. 1 Corinthians 7:3 (NKJV) and 4) Terry submits to her husband, as to the Lord. For the husband is head of the wife, as also Christ is the head of the church … so let Terry be subject to her own husband in everything. Terry's husband loves her just as Christ loved the Church and gave Himself for her, that he might sanctify and cleanse her with the washing of the Word. Ephesians 5:22-26 (NKJV)

Lloyd responded, "Terry, these are beautiful confessions. I'm in full alignment with them and with the need for continual prayer to bring them into existence. In faith, I will replace 'Terry's husband' with 'Lloyd'."

My purpose for sharing my confessions with him was to join hearts and be on one accord with where the relationship was headed. The word of God says, "Again, truly I tell you that if two of you on earth agree about anything they ask for, it will be done for them by my Father in heaven. For where two or three gather in my name, there am I with them." Matthew 18: 19-20 (NIV) I invited God into our relationship early on – my desire was that our relationship and marriage be like a threefold cord, God-Lloyd-me, which is not easily broken.

Dreams Do Come True

We got engaged on December 25 that same year and married the following April. After becoming engaged, some of the many details of being married that we discussed beforehand included: what church we would attend; our finances and who would manage the budget; having more children and would I continue working; and we also attended pre-marital counseling at his church.

I recall from our first counseling session what the pastor told us, which was if at any time either of us decided that things were not working out during our engagement and wedding planning that it was not too late to break off the engagement. He stated that we should not be deterred by how much money or time had been spent on the wedding, and reiterated that it is better to break off an engagement than to go forth with a wedding, and then get a divorce. It was at this moment that I fully realized how close I was to being married and the finality of my journey to being married. The year that encompassed the time that I met, dated, became engaged, and got married is all surreal to me. After so many years of preparation, I almost could not believe that marriage was about to actually happen for me.

A final highlight of our premarital counseling is a statement that the pastor made to us as we approached one of our final sessions, he stated that our marriage would be a billboard for God that would advertise to the world that marriage is a good thing and it works.

I Am Ruth

Throughout my courtship and dating Lloyd, God was constantly reminding me that He had heard my every cry, all of my prayers, and all of my pleas while I was single. I remember a point in our exchange of vows during our wedding ceremony where I was poignantly reminded of God's presence in my situation. As I shared previously, while I was single I often read the book of Ruth to find strength and encouragement.

While reciting my part of the wedding vow, there was a line in the vow where I stated, "…where you go, I will go; wherever you live, I will live. Your people will be my people, and your God will be my God…" at that point, I almost lost it. I became overwhelmed with emotion. I realized that God used the very scripture that I found strength in during my season of singleness as part of my wedding ceremony. This scripture not only carried me through my season of singleness but bridged the pathway to a new season in my life – me as a wife.

CHAPTER 19

FINAL WORD OF ENCOURAGEMENT

A Season for Everything

The word of God says that "everything has a time" Ecclesiastes 3:1, "To everything there is a season, A time for every purpose under heaven: ..." (NKJV) For those of you desiring to be married, there is indeed a time, a season for preparation. For every woman, that season is different. For some ladies, preparation for marriage may be a few months and for others—like me—it is several years. As you begin your process of preparation—and after reading this book—my prayer is that you will outline areas of your life that you need to deal with. Ask God daily to guide and lead you down your path of living a joyous, meaningful single life. You must first of all love and appreciate you before anyone else will.

I encourage you to not get weary in well-doing for there is an ordained season for singleness and an ordained season to be married. Use your season of singleness to prepare yourself for the husband that God has ordained for you. Use this time of preparation to work on you. Don't just strive for the goal of getting to the Lady-in-Waiting, but strive to adorn yourself in a spirit of holiness that will not only attract the man of God that your heart desires, but more importantly the man of God that God desires for you. Don't allow vain desires to keep you from what God has for you. God knows the desires of your heart but more importantly He knows what's best for you and He has not forgotten about you. He wants you to be in the right position to be blessed.

Just like Sarah (Genesis 21:6 NKJV), God wants to bless you at a level that you will literally be overwhelmed with laughter and the people around you will rejoice and laugh with you.

PART IV: SURVEY RESULTS

CHAPTER 20

SINGLE LADIES SURVEY

RESULTS SUMMARY

As I was finishing up the initial rough draft for this book, I felt led to do a survey geared toward single women and to get their views on divorce, dating, and their overall stance on being single. I wanted to get a deeper understanding of the seven personalities of the single women. I sent the survey to just over 100 family, friends, and colleagues who were single and married and asked them to forward the survey to their network of single ladies. I received 34 surveys back, which is a 34% return rate, an approximation considering, I cannot confirm how many people actually forwarded the survey and to how many people. This chapter summarizes my survey findings.

Demographics

Age

The age range for the ladies was 25 – 70 years of age. The majority of the surveys that were returned were from ladies in their forties (50%). The next biggest group was from ladies in their thirties (21%), then twenties (14%).

Education

Most of the ladies who returned the survey had a master's degree (43%), the second biggest group had some college (36%); and there were ladies who had a bachelor's degree and others who had completed high school.

Marital Status

Of the respondents, about half had been married before, and the other half had never been married. For those who had been married, most had been married between 3 and 12 years; one respondent had been married for longer than 20 years.

Stance on Divorce

Overall, the ladies did not believe in divorce, unless it was for a serious issue such as infidelity or incompatibility. For those respondents who were divorced, the top reason listed for their divorce was infidelity, the second lack of communication, and the third most common reason was incompatibility.

"I do believe in divorce for issues such as infidelity. In other cases like finances I believe most cases could be worked out." **A survey respondent**

View on Dating

The responses regarding dating varied. Some women did not like dating. Others felt like dating with boundaries and a purpose was okay. Yet others were okay with casual dating and friendship. One respondent stated that she had not dated since her divorce.

"I believe dating is another word for putting myself on the modern day threshing floor and if it so happens that a man is drawn to my light and glory and wants to befriend me, then I do not see an issue with dating as long as it does not take me outside of giving God glory." **A survey respondent**

"Everyone should have someone from the opposite sex in their life for friendship, relationships, conversation, travel, and partnering to attend theaters, plays, and sports events. It helps one keep a balance within." **A survey respondent**

Why Are You Single?

The survey responses to the question asking, "Why are you single?" were varied. Responses ranged from "single by choice" to "single due to the death of a spouse."

"I want to be single for the moment." **A survey respondent**

"God's plan for this season and I'm working on healing and deliverance (being whole). When process complete, marriage will happen." **A survey respondent**

"It hasn't been part of God's plan for my life up until now. I never envision proposing to a man, and no one has asked me to marry them. So far, considering past relationships, it has been for the best." **A survey respondent**

"I do not want to marry again." **A survey respondent**

"By choice." **A survey respondent**

"Death of a husband. I'm not single by choice. I haven't found anyone of compatible interest." **A survey respondent**

Feelings about Being Single

Several ladies responded that they loved being single because they truly enjoy their freedom.

"Not that big of a deal, at times I do get lonely, but then I pop out of that and get refocused and get busy. I'm enjoying my peace of mind (hallelujah) and independence and freedom ... it's GREAT ..." **A survey respondent**

"It is not my choice or desire, but I must trust God." **A survey respondent**

"It's okay. I've learned to be content in whatever state I'm in." **A survey respondent**

"I feel fine. One less person I have to be bothered with." **A survey respondent**

Top Three Characteristics a Husband Must Possess

When asked about the top three characteristics their husband must possess, the top three responses were 1) relationship with God, 2) honesty, and 3) sense of humor. The sense of humor response was a little surprising. I was surprised that this characteristic ranked so highly for several of the women surveyed.

Other characteristics that were listed included trustworthy, ambitious, good provider, employed, supportive, good personality, loving, accepting, family oriented, work oriented, communicator, financially stable, compatible, faithful, neat, healthy/fit, respectful, and love/accept my child(ren).

Categorize Yourself and Explain Why

When asked to categorize themselves into one of the six characteristics presented, most women stated that they were Career Women. The second highest responses were tied between Professional Student and Single Parent. And the third most common response was a

Church Sister.

One respondent stated, *"Single Parent – because I allowed an unworthy man to intervene in my 'Church Sister' relationship."* Other responses included:

"Career Woman – I've moved up quickly in my career, moved around and abroad, and on the fast track for upward growth."

"Church Sister – just not looking – I figured if God wants me to have or find a mate it will happen in time."

"Church Sister – I am dating Jesus; I have no problems."

ABOUT THE AUTHOR

No Longer a Bridesmaid! is a memoir that chronicles the seven years that Terry Cato was single and preparing herself to be a wife and mother. When she came of age and decided that she wanted to be married, she soon realized that she did not have any positive examples of what a successful marriage looked liked – everyone close to her had experienced divorce. One of her cousins gave her a book that encouraged singles to begin preparing themselves for marriage while they are single. Thus, Terry began her journey of preparation, healing, and deliverance.

Terry Cato is an entrepreneur and community volunteer. She is married to Lloyd. They have two daughters and one son and reside in the San Francisco Bay Area. An avid reader, for as long as she can remember, she has always had a love for reading and writing. She wrote sentences in her coloring books before she would color the pages in grade school and began writing song and rap lyrics as an adolescent. She has written poems, essays, and song lyrics. Terry attended the University of Southern Mississippi and obtained her undergraduate degree in marketing and a master's degree in sports administration from the United States Sports Academy. She has worked in the professional sports and non-profit industries.

To invite her to speak at your women's retreat, conference, convention, or other event, email her at booking@terrycato.com.

CONNECT WITH THE AUTHOR

Blog: www.terry411cato.com

Website: www.terrycato.com

Twitter: https://twitter.com/terry411cato